Moments of Excess

Movements, protest and everyday life

Moments of Excess: Movements, protest and everyday life
The Free Association
© 2011 by PM Press
All rights reserved. No part of this book may be transmitted by any means without
permission in writing from the publisher.

ISBN: 978-1-60486-113-6
Library of Congress Control Number: 2010916474

Cover and interior design by briandesign

10 9 8 7 6 5 4 3 2 1

PM Press
PO Box 23912
Oakland, CA 94623
www.pmpress.org

Printed in the USA on recycled paper.

to George, Jack, Lisa, Mae, Fred, Eve, Rohan and Eliza

Contents

Introduction

The texts collected here were written over a ten year period from summer 2001 to January 2011. All were initially written as interventions, one way or another, so it's no surprise that they betray their origin and context. One or two were originally written for books, some appeared in 'movement' publications such as *Derive Approdi* and *Turbulence*, and most were also handed out as self-published booklets in the heat of the moment. Yet as we assembled this edition, we were struck by how well the articles hang together as a collection. They are coherent—and they tell a story.

But before we think about what that story might be, there are a couple of points worth making. First, we write from a European perspective. More precisely, as we explain in 'What is the movement?', we write from a UK standpoint that is itself rooted in several different traditions. That doesn't mean that we're not internationalists. Far from it. But our writing starts where we are, which has been (mostly) within northern Europe. Allied to this, we don't claim to represent any position within contemporary anti-capitalist politics—indeed any claim to 'represent' a movement is a dangerous distortion: at best, a movement can only be *sampled*. In many respects, the trajectory revealed in this book is ours alone.

But this disclaimer must be qualified by the second, more important point which is that our writing has always been collective. At the outset, this approach seemed almost incidental, but over time it has become increasingly central to who we are and the way we work. Collective writing is a strange process, in equal parts painful and liber-

ating. At the most immediate level, there's little room for ego or posturing because there's always someone on hand to cut you down to
size. But the physical process of writing is itself far more complex. Our
articles begin as group discussions which span several sessions and
locations. The drafts that follow are circulated and discussed, often
among a much wider network, and then re-edited so many times that
no-one can claim authorship of any one insight or line. The end product is richer, more complex and far more nuanced than anything we
could produce individually.

So what is the story of *Moments of Excess*? Re-reading these texts,
at least three different narratives emerge from the threads that run
through them. One is a tale about the movement of movements,
focused on the cycle of counter-summit mobilisations that is usually
reckoned to have begun with the WTO Seattle meeting in November
1999 (but which can actually be traced back to the Global Street Party
which greeted the 1998 G8 summit in Birmingham and the J18 Carnival
Against Capital the following year). At the time of writing, there is a
clear sense that this cycle has come to an end—first stalled and then
definitively thrown aside by the economic crisis that ripped across the
planet in 2008. One of the key questions raised in this period is the way
intensive collective experiences—moments of excess—relate to everyday life. As those mobilisations expanded, we also began to think about
the relationship between the problematics thrown up by social movements and the demands that they appear to express.

But while it's possible to track the changing shape of the movement of movements in this collection, the reality is much more messy.
For one thing, cycles of struggle don't begin and end as neatly as we
might like, so the lineages we propose—from anarcho-punk to Seattle,
for example—are entirely subjective, related to our own political and
personal histories. Again, while some detect a brand new politics in
the anti-austerity struggles now emerging across Europe, others rightly
point to the battles which raged in Africa against IMF-imposed structural adjustment programmes in the 1980s. So there is a second, wider
thread here about the form of politics appropriate to the world we live
in. Neoliberalism's ideology of permanent progress through growth
may have been shattered by the economic crisis, but it staggers on,
zombie-like—and unprecedented cuts in public expenditure across the
world are actually expanding its programme of social decomposition.
As cracks appear in the most unlikely of places, there's space to ask
the one question worth asking: *what sort of world do we want to live in?*

Finally there is a much older narrative in these pages, the story of 'the old mole that can work in the earth so fast'.[1] As we say in 'What is a life?':

> These are whispers across time and space that can't be silenced. However it's expressed—'*Omnia sunt communia*', 'The poor shall wear the crown', '*Que se vayan todos*'—we hear the same refusal, the same desire to stop the world as we know it and create something else.

Who knows? By tomorrow, this collection may well be meaningless, rendered irrelevant by the grubbing of that old mole. We are, after all, part of 'the real movement which abolishes the present state of things'.

Leeds
January 2011

Anti-capitalist movements

Communism is not for us a state of affairs which is to be established, an ideal to which reality [will] have to adjust itself. We call communism the real movement, which abolishes the present state of things.[1]

WHAT'S MY NAME?

From Seattle to Gothenburg and Genoa, from Evian and Gleneagles, and from Argentina 2001 to France 2006, a new movement has come into existence: and one of the labels to which it has been attached is 'anti-capitalist'. We should not underestimate the significance of this terminology. Following years of defeat and disarray among oppositional movements, we've enjoyed new-found energy and experienced moments which have punctured the world of money and power. Once again we can just make out the spectre of communism haunting the world.

But what does it mean to talk of an 'anti-capitalist movement'? What do we mean by the word 'movement'? Its most straightforward meaning is a collection of individuals connected by means of some shared ideology or practice. This new anti-capitalist movement is, then, quite simply composed of those individuals who are consciously, collectively and actively opposed to capitalism. By this definition, it clearly includes those who danced in the streets at the J18 Carnival against Capitalism in London in 1999, and those who took to the streets of Genoa and Gothenburg in 2001. But beyond this things get more problematic. The movement may also include those on the streets of Seattle in 1999, but would it also incorporate those who attempted to defend Nike stores from the violence of some of the Seattle demonstrators? More recently, where can we place those who took part in the Make Poverty History mobilisations of 2005? Or those who went to the Live8 concerts? Or Bob Geldof and Bono?

Even such a simple understanding of 'the movement' soon starts to unravel. For one thing, it quickly falls into the trap of playing the numbers game: this many demonstrators, that much damage. As one contributor to *Reflections on J18* sarcastically notes: 'we congratulate ourselves through commodifying our resistance, 2 million quid of damage—good demo!'[2] It's an approach that tends to exclude those who can't or won't attend the big spectacular demonstrations and actions, or who aren't even aware of their happening. In fact it dovetails neatly into the recruitment practices of much of the organised left, as well as the 'activist' mentality of many in the current movement. Both perspectives suggest that just one more paper-sale, one more demonstration, one more action can tip the balance decisively in our favour, as if a real qualitative transformation of our lives will be simply a matter of quantitative change. Despite their protestations to the contrary, both are driven by the same underlying attitudes:

> The activist is a specialist or an expert in social change. To think of yourself as being an activist means to think of yourself as being somehow privileged or more advanced than others in your appreciation of the need for social change, in the knowledge of how to achieve it and as leading or being in the forefront of the practical struggle to create this change...
>
> Defining ourselves as activists means defining our actions as the ones which will bring about social change, thus disregarding the activity of thousands upon thousands of other non-activists. Activism is based upon this misconception that it is only activists who do social change.[3]

A further problem with this numbers approach is that it tends to be Eurocentric, and almost always privileges those groups that have been identified in advance as 'political formations', regardless of whether such groups style themselves as an 'organisation' or 'party' (for example, the Socialist Workers Party), a 'network' (for example, People's Global Action), a 'disorganisation' (for example, Reclaim the Streets) or something even looser. In fact the vast bulk of the movement is made up of people who do not consider themselves 'activists' or 'political' but who nevertheless have to struggle against oppression and exploitation in their everyday lives—people who, just like us, are struggling for new ways of living.

However, simply expanding the definition of movement—to include millions of workers and peasants and any other number of social groupings across the world—is still limited by the fact that it conceives of movement as 'a thing'. As something that can be defined, whose boundaries can be clearly mapped, and which stands *outside* and *against* something else called 'capital'. We may argue over the exact terms of the definition (for example, do we include Make Poverty History?) and we may agree that these definitions will shift but this movement is still seen as a *thing*. It is increasingly difficult, though, to reconcile such a static, thing-like view of the anti-capitalist movement with the realities of everyday life—not least our own—where the vast majority of the world's population exists both *within* and *against* capital.

In trying to rethink this, we have drawn heavily on our own political experiences (mainly but not exclusively within the libertarian revolutionary milieu) and on the analysis developed by so-called autonomist Marxists. We have found two aspects of the autonomists' analyses particularly helpful: first, the idea of workers' autonomy—the potential autonomy of labour from capital—and, second, the understanding that 'capital is nothing other than the *product* of the working class'[4] and hence, as we mentioned above, we exist *within-and-against* capital.

While many orthodox Marxists emphasise the power of capital, taking at face value the 'inevitable' unfolding of its laws, this first insight—that of workers' autonomy—reverses the perspective entirely. It instead asserts the primacy of *working-class struggle* and recasts capital in a reactive role. As one of its earliest theorists puts it:

> We too have worked with a concept that puts capitalist development first, and workers second. This is a mistake. And now we have to turn the problem on its head, reverse the polarity, and start again from the beginning: and the beginning is the class struggle of the working class. At the level of socially developed capital, capitalist development becomes subordinated to working class struggles; it follows behind them, and they set the pace to which the political mechanisms of capital's own reproduction must be tuned.[5]

If the first insight reverses the polarity between capital and labour, the second attempts to dissolve this polarity entirely. Instead of seeing capital as a 'thing' external to the working class, the relationship between capital and labour is viewed as *internal*. Fundamental is the view, developed from Marx, of capital as a social relation, one that contains labour within it. As Marx characterises workers:

> Their co-operation only begins with the labour process, but by then they have ceased to belong to themselves. On entering the labour process they are incorporated into capital. As co-operators, as members of a working organism, they merely form a particular mode of existence of capital. **Hence the productive power developed by the worker socially is the productive power of capital.**[6]

'Capital' is not something 'out there', something that we can fight against as if it were external to us and part of someone or something else—even if we sometimes talk about it as if it is. 'Capital' is not a person or group of people, nor an organisation or group of organisations. It's not the sum total of 'capitalists' or 'capitalist enterprises'. Capital is a social relation mediated through commodities. Capital is the way we live, the way we reproduce ourselves and our world—the entire organisation of the 'present state of things' as they are today.

But capital is reliant on the expenditure of our labour to valorise itself. What lies under capitalist development is the social production of co-operative labour. While labour can never be autonomous from capital, through its constant insubordination it tries to affirm itself as the social subject beyond capital. Conversely capital constantly tries to contain the working class within the limits of its form as a mere living container of labour power, reducing the whole of life to work— for the sake of work. This forms the fundamental cycle of what is termed 'class composition': our autonomous struggles provoke capital to restructure the production process and the division of labour in order to reassert its command. This in turn leads to the development of new antagonistic subjectivities, a 'recomposition' of the working class, not as a wage-labouring class demanding a better, new deal, but as the multitude-in-resistance that demands the end of class. The only possibilities of escape from this cycle of decomposition and recomposition, of imposition of work and resistance to this imposition, lie in the asymmetry at the heart of the relationship between capital and labour: while capital needs labour, labour does not need capital. Instead of the familiar view of capitalism as confident and monolithic, we are left with a picture of a social order constantly forced to recompose itself in attempt to co-opt, channel and cap the 'creative unrest' of human labour.

In short, it is human practice—what we do—which is central. Although we do not choose our conditions, nevertheless we do, collectively, make our own history: 'Human beings make their own history ... not under circumstances they themselves have chosen but under the given and inherited circumstances with which they are directly confronted.'[7] Or, as the graffiti in Genoa expressed it: 'You make plans. We make history!' Orthodox Marxist thinking has tended to read off human action as a function of class, or as a function of some other social category. But if human practice—doing—is central, then we should begin with the doing. Class and 'movement' then become truly dynamic categories which develop with the doing. As an English historian put it, '[class] is an *historical* phenomenon. I do not see [it] as a "structure", nor even as a "category", but as something which in fact happens (and can be shown to have happened) in human relationships.'[8] Or, in the words of *autonomia*: 'We don't start with the class: we come to it. Or better, we reach a new level of class composition. We begin with struggle ... We go from the struggle to the class.'[9]

It is far more fruitful then to conceive of movements as the moving of these social relations of struggle—in crude terms, movements not of people, but of people *doing things*: that is, the multitude-in-practice. This dynamic approach allows us to sidestep many of the traps that lie in wait for more orthodox theorists. For instance, from this perspective what people do is far more important than what they say. We no longer have to rely on people's own self-definition ('I'm a communist, therefore everything I do is anti-capitalist'). Communism is, after all, not a label but critical, purposeful social practice.

Moreover, if movements are the *moving* of social relations of struggle, it no longer makes sense to talk of static boundaries or limits ('these people are in the anti-capitalist movement, those people aren't...'). But it makes no more sense to adopt a simple anti-identity position (one which would itself offer an 'identity'). Living a life will always involve some sort of definition, however temporary and tentative, if only to ward off entropy. More crucially, social movements (the moving of social relations) travel through moments of expansion and contraction. In this, the act of drawing boundaries, of defining ourselves in some way, can prove immensely productive, by generating further moments of expansion as we fight to overcome the limits we have set ourselves. In the UK, the trajectory of the anti-roads movement is a good example. What started out as an 'environmentalist' struggle in the early 1990s became an explicitly 'anti-capitalist' one within a few years, not through a conscious adoption of a communist ideology but simply because people's practices kept coming up against, and *overcoming*, the limits set by capital.

Finally, the dynamic approach to 'movement' opens our eyes to the everyday activities, both individual and collective, of millions upon millions of 'ordinary' people. Closer to our own political histories we can start to see how, in the rush to abandon the 'lifestylism' and 'single issue politics' that were so predominant in the mid to late 1980s, many of us also jettisoned its actual social practices—practices which were in retrospect far more radical than those of the more formal 'revolutionary' groups (in our case Class War) to which we gravitated.[10] Here we can also see a way out of the traditional 'means and ends' dichotomy. Historically anti-capitalist movements have too often thrown up organisational forms which ran counter to their long-term objectives. We only need to glance at the history of the 'communist' movement in the twentieth century, for example, to see party being put before class with devastating consequences. This is a theme to which we will return later.

LOST IN THE SUPERMARKET

Anti-capitalist movements, then, are movements of social relations. As such they occur across a number of dimensions, both spatial and temporal. One of the key characteristics about the current movement is its immediately global nature. In this respect 'globalisation', far from being a one-sided extension of capital's power, entangling the whole world in the logic of the market, is actually a response to the flexing of our muscles in the 1960s and 1970s—which temporarily forced capital on to the defensive. From capital's perspective globalisation is an inevitable corollary of its ceaseless self-expansion. From our perspective it is as much a *flight from* our insubordination as a *flight to* new untapped markets.[11] And here it is useful to think of circuits of struggle, of the ways in which struggles in one country reverberate and are amplified around the world. This process can occur simultaneously at a number of levels—for instance, the Zapatista uprising, besides inspiring many thousands, even millions, around the globe, gave birth to the *encuentros*, which in turn inspired many similar events across the globe. On another level, labour militancy in, say, South Korea may cause some sectors of capital to relocate to South Wales, while other elements move to Seoul to assist in decomposition of the class there. Of course, as some have argued, the current 'anti-globalisation' tag is a misnomer:

'it should not be called an anti-globalisation movement. It is pro-glo-balisation, or rather an alternative globalisation movement, one that seeks to expand the possibilities of self-determination'.[12] The current phase of globalisation is a real response by capital to our own ongoing dissension and revolt across the world, to the ways in which we have attempted to undermine the capital relation, to refashion social rela-tions in our own interests.

Movements of social relations also occur across time. It may appear a truism, but anti-capitalist movements of the early twentieth cen-tury are vastly different from those of the present day. Again, just as at a global level, what we see here is the operation of that spiralling 'double helix' identified by Tronti: working-class composition and cap-italist restructuring chase each other over the span of historical peri-ods in ever more complex ways. More specifically, we can reconsider Negri's historical phases of capitalist development in the light of our new understanding of movement. At the risk of being over-schematic, Negri identifies three broad phases. First we have the era of the 'pro-fessional worker', which we might characterise as running from the middle of the nineteenth century to the outbreak of World War One. This is the 'classic' period of large scale industry which sees the dom-inance of productive factory labour ('skilled workers') and the forma-tion of the first workers' political parties. The second phase is the age of the 'mass worker', which we could say runs from 1918 to the late 1960s. This phase is characterised by increasingly alienated work pro-cesses (Taylorism), mechanisation and mass production (Fordism), and a heavily interventionist State model (Keynesianism). The third, cur-rent, phase is that of the 'socialised worker'. In this phase the factory is dispersed into society, giving rise to the 'social factory' and the 'real subsumption' of social labour under capital.

In the era of the professional worker, capitalist command and con-trol is based firmly within the factory, and outside of this there are areas which are left relatively untouched (although that is not to say they were havens of peace and freedom as they were subject to other forms of hierarchy and domination). We can see the transition from this era to that of the mass worker as a result of, on the one hand, labour's flight *of* insubordination and, on the other, capital's flight *from* insubordination. Through its struggles over the length of the working day and over 'skills', labour sought to escape the discipline of the fac-tory. Capital, in its turn, was forced to respond on two fronts. Within the factory, it sought to flee labour's insubordination by 'displacing' workers with machines and by increasing its control over the remaining labour-power with those self-same machines. But capital can only exist through labour, through dominating living labour. As labour fled the factory, capital was forced—to secure its very existence—to pursue it and thus developed the political, economic and social strategies associated with the era of the mass worker.

Turning now to the late 1960s and '70s, the transition from the era of the mass worker to that of the socialised worker, we can see how this too was a product of the flight of and from insubordination, as the movement of the capital relation. Throughout society, insubordinate labour refused capitalist domination. While factory workers practised strikes, go-slows and industrial sabotage, there was an explosion of new social movements, typified by the rise of the Black Power, women's and lesbian and gay rights movements, and importantly also the anti-nuclear movement of the 1970s. Some factory workers, besides demanding more money and less work, experimented with alternative uses for the factory; the new social subjects fiercely proclaimed their autonomy, their difference, their individual and collective identities; beyond the factory floor, all the activities associated with the 'counter-culture' were nothing other than explorations in new ways of being. Once more, capital was forced to flee, yet also to chase. Taking flight from insubordinate waged workers in the North, it has relocated much physical production to the South and East.[13] And it has 'taken on' the counter-culture, commodifying what previously appeared unruly and domesticating 'dissent' by making it a profitable and marketable asset in the burgeoning 'culture industry'. Labour power as a category and capitalist command is extended throughout society to such an extent that it now makes sense to see the whole of society functioning as a moment of production. Time for ourselves is increasingly time spent either preparing for work or time spent engaging in 'leisure'—regimented forms of 'free time' that seem closer to break time at school than periods when we can decide what we really might want to do with our lives. In short, capital is now entirely social and its power is almost completely diffuse throughout every level of society. Negri captured this development well when he argued that 'productive labour is no longer "that which directly produces capital", but that which reproduces society'.[14]

Of course it is important to recognise that the most modern and technological expressions of this 'social factory' sit side by side with more brutal forms of capitalist domination. No matter what the hype says, we are not all web designers now, and in some parts of the world capital is still attempting to carry out the enclosures and expropriation of common land that it enforced in the UK over three hundred years ago. Elements of 'primitive' and 'developed' are frequently intimately entangled: the new technology worker's lunch-time latte is made by close-to-minimum-wage employees, while the metallic ores—cobalt, copper, coltan—which end up in computers, cell phones and other electronic equipment are frequently mined in conditions that would have been unthinkable even in the darkest hours of the pre-Chartist nineteenth century. But even where capital is struggling to impose itself, it's impossible to deny that capital is starting to suffuse all forms of social life: when TV images show those resisting expropriation are wearing last year's Nike cast-offs from the West, how can the principled distinctions of the past be maintained?

In this nightmare vision of invisible, even 'totalitarian' control, it might appear hard to see what space is left for anti-capitalist movements. But if capital is primarily a social (class) relation, and if the capital relation is a global relation, then capital is contested everywhere. Or, in a neater summation, '[t]he proletariat is everywhere, just as the boss is'.[15] A vicious circle develops: because capital is so diffuse, so the sites of resistance and antagonism become generalised and diverse—and are automatically social. In contrast to the earlier periods, the state's primary role is now one of decomposition, of neutralising our resistance to capital, rather than one of mediation. Thatcherism and Reaganomics were just early expressions of this deep structural shift. Low intensity conflicts and 'slow riots' are the order of the day—'low intensity' both because they rumble on and on without end and, crucially, because there are no longer any Winter Palaces to storm. In fact the real subsumption of labour under capital means that there is no space left between capitalism and anti-capitalism—there is no 'outside' any more, if indeed there ever was. So while capital might appear stronger than ever, its grip is more precarious than ever. Without the safety valves of the past, everything now goes straight to the heart of its mode of domination. As one of our former Class War comrades succinctly put it, 'There's now only one question worth asking: what sort of world do we want to live in?' This formulation is echoed elsewhere: 'How are we to become what we already are?'[16]; and: 'What is it to live in a society completely constituted on the basis of freedom?'[17] It is on this basis that a whole new anti-capitalist politics has started to flourish.

COMPLETE CONTROL

With the development of the social factory, the entire terrain of politics has shifted to what could be described as the abstract and the universal. Capital has 'socialised' itself to escape the battles we waged in the factory, and in so doing has unwittingly opened the way for a new form of politics ('postpolitical politics' in Surin's words). For us the key issue here is not just the emergence of a self-defined 'anti-capitalist' movement. It is also the real experimentation with social practices and organisational forms that can prove adequate to the task. Here we think of the tendency to develop horizontal networks, non-hierarchical information and skills exchanges; the imaginative attempts to move beyond sterile, ossified positions (e.g. the efforts of *Tute Bianche* (White Overalls) to transcend the violence/non-violence issues in Genoa); the shift to more flexible, informal ways of organising; the rejection of representation (other people doing things on our behalf) in favour of direct action; the reintroduction of notions of pleasure and fun into 'politics'; the increasing recognition of our vulnerability as human beings and attempts meet the need that spring from that (as shown by the Activist-Trauma support group at Gleneagles); and, above all, the willingness to be open and honest, to think sideways, and to do things differently. As De Angelis has pointed out, two interdependent fronts have been opened up: 'one is of the limit to capital, and therefore against the limit that capital places upon us—the other is that of relations with the other, a network based on respect, dignity and direct democracy.'[18] This simultaneous struggle *against* capital and *for* new, unexplored and diverse ways of being is encapsulated in the Zapatista slogan 'One *No*, Many *Yeses*'. That is to say, the 'anti-capitalist movements' fight on the one hand *against* capital, and on the other *for* us. And it is the shift to the second front which seems to be the most decisive. Having created a space from where we can start to pose limits to capital, we have also created a space from where we can start to create situations which go beyond capital. Here we return to Marx's formulation from his *German Ideology* with which we began, or as it has been more recently expressed:

> The aim is not to force the creation of something which has never existed but to free those forces which already exist, to 'develop potentialities slumbering within' existing social being. The task is to discover, hidden inside the chaos of modern life, the elements of a set of relations between human beings, including their relations with the natural world, which are 'worthy of their human nature.'[19]

From this perspective, anti-capitalist movements are concerted attempts to discover what we already are.

However, we need to introduce a note of caution. Neat as this scheme might appear, it would be foolish (and dangerous) to mistake the map for the territory. Anti-capitalist movements at particular points in time throw up new forms of political organisation, but these organisational forms also have a life and a power of their own. They quickly become limits which react back upon the real movements of social relations from where they arose—the Bolshevik model, for example, is an organisational practice which still has an enormously damaging effect on our ability to organise ourselves effectively against capital.[20] In this respect, it's possible to talk of a third front opening up, one against outdated and alienating political forms. After the attempted criminalisation of the entire movement in Genoa, and increased repression and marginalisation by the 'war on terror', there has been pressure on the movement to define itself, to offer up its programme for inspection and negotiation. Crucially, part of this pressure has come from 'within' the movement, from political organisations which can only think in terms of 'demands', 'lobbying' and more of the same old mediation.[21] Outright repression and clumsy attempts to freeze and channel these movements of social relations both belong to the same strategy of enclosure. In refusing to be defined and limited, we both defend and deepen a process that represents the dynamic, self-expanding unfolding of our power—a real attempt to work out in practical terms new ways of being.

What is the movement?

(BY WAY OF AN) INTRODUCTION
We'll start by introducing ourselves. We are five people, one woman and four men, living in or close to Leeds, a large city in the north of England. We all work as 'immaterial labourers'—health, education, information and design. We have all known each other for at least four years; four of us have been working together politically for more than a decade. We are comrades, but as important, we are friends and these seem inseparable: when we have 'political' meetings we also gossip, when we meet socially we frequently talk 'politics'.

We share a background in the 'anarchist movement'. The four of us who have known each other longest were all members of the national anarchist group Class War, which published the newspaper of the same name. We were part of determined minority which successfully argued for the dissolution of this organisation (in 1997), on the grounds that it had outlived its usefulness and was unable to relate to exciting new forms of struggle, such as the anti-roads movement. Following this we helped organised a conference, Bradford May Day '98, to discuss 'the situation' in the UK—failure of revolutionary groups, the new forms of protest, etc. The conference both was grounded in the events surrounding Class War's dissolution and was inspired by the Intercontinental Encounters for Humanity and Against Neoliberalism (the *encuentros*), held in 1996 (in Chiapas, Mexico) and in 1997 (in Spain). The Bradford conference attracted several hundred anarchists, both aligned and non-aligned, communists and activists. We met our fifth member at this conference.

Attempting to sustain the success of Bradford '98, we continued organising 'open' discussion meetings on a local basis, but these never really took off. Following the London May Day 2000 conference, the five of us agreed to meet regularly as a reading group. So, for the past two years, we have been meeting regularly, reading and discussing pamphlets, articles and books, most notably the first volume of Marx's *Capital*, and gaining numerous insights into the way we live. We have attempted to express ourselves in the written word, but have had much more mixed success with this.

THE LIST OF 'PROBLEMS'

First off, we think the events and processes described in *Derive Approdi*'s 'open letter to the European movements' are enormously important and they have certainly helped shaped our own politics. We share the excitement as we witness what appears to be the emergence of a new movement, one which, moreover describes itself—and is described—as 'anti-capitalist'. It seems significant that so many diverse social group-ings are coming together both to seek common ground and to explore differences. A decade ago, for example, we personally would have been scathing of the involvement of pacifists, Greens, Christians and anyone from a left-wing party. Now, we are much more open to the possibil-ities as such people communicate with those, like ourselves, from a more historically radical or antagonistic tradition. We have also noted the increasing politicisation of a new generation. What is more, this politicisation seems faster than in 'our day', this due, we think, to the decline of many of the old forms of mediation—grassroots-based social democratic parties (the Labour Party), trades unions, etc. It is as if we are witnessing 'fast-track' revolutionaries: today reading *No Logo*, tomorrow boycotting McDonald's and the day after that hurling a rock through its windows and fighting with the police.

However, we find it hard to relate other than tangentially to many of the questions in the list of problems. The main reason for this is that the questions implicitly adopt an understanding of 'movement' which increasingly makes less and less sense to us. We'll try and explain what we mean by tracing the development of our thought over the past decade or so.

1992–97

For us, our ideas have been transformed by a number of struggles throughout the 1990s. Most notably, we have been influenced by the anti-roads movement, the free-festival/free-party movement and the campaign against the government's Criminal Justice Bill (CJB), which infamously defined techno as music 'characterised by a series of repetitive beats'. Two aspects of these struggles stood out.

First, the emphasis on having a good time, on laughter, their quality of being not only against capital, but also of going beyond capital. Thus, Reclaim the Streets (RTS) not only closed off roads to motor traffic, they provided sound systems so people could dance in the streets. Demonstrations against the CJB took the form of massive street parties, rather than boring marches: people dressed up and danced. They were fun! Whereas old-style left marches seemed to be purely about demonstrating our Power to some external opponent, these events were in addition an experiment into possible future ways of living. Reclaim the Streets events did not demand the closure of roads, they did close them. We were exercising power!

Second, by and large, the subjects of these struggles were not traditional 'politicos'. Few had backgrounds in the anarchist scene or left parties or campaigns. Most people who attended and organised free parties and festivals (find a field or forest clearing, arrange a sound system and a DJ or two, get the word out) simply wanted to dance and have a good time without having to fork out (pay) a lot of money. But they became politicised when the state clamped down, outlawing and breaking up parties, and introducing the CJB. Some of these people even seemed to be 'middle class'.

In fact, it was partly because of the unusual social composition of these struggles that many on the left, including many in Class War, were unable to take these struggles seriously. This was ironic in the case of Class War, since what made Class War so unusual, when it was first published in 1984, was its emphasis on workers' power, both against and beyond capital. Most left newspapers, in contrast, saw only victims. The orthodox left's failure to comprehend these new struggles seemed to be based in its prioritising of identity over practice. Thus a few in Class War championed lorry drivers over anti-roads protestors, since the former were 'working class', whilst the latter were 'middle-class students'. They did not see the importance of transport, in general, and new roads, in particular, to capitalist restructuring (neoliberalism). They therefore found it hard to understand that the doing of opposing new roads was a directly anti-capital doing.

One of the highpoints of this struggle was the March for Social Justice/Never Mind the Ballots, a massive street party in London just before the 1997 General Election. The event was the result of a collaboration between Reclaim the Streets and the sacked Liverpool Dockers. This collaboration was significant since it representing the meeting of two very different social groupings and forms of struggle. Reclaim the Streets parties, in London and throughout the UK, have continued throughout the second half of the 1990s.

1998–2002

Over the past five years, we have a witnessed a growing cycle of international protests: in 1998, against the G8 summit in Birmingham; a year later, events worldwide for J18 and N30 (most notably Seattle); more worldwide events on May Day 2000, followed by demonstrations against the IMF and World Bank at their September meeting in Prague; more demonstrations worldwide on May Day 2001, then protests against the EU summit in Gothenburg in June and against the G8 summit in Genoa in July; and so on. These international protests seem to have heralded the emergence of a new movement against capital, a movement which seemed to be rapidly gathering momentum (at least until September 11).

On the one hand, we have been totally inspired by this series of protests. But, on the other, they started to leave us feeling rather uncomfortable. We ourselves have been reluctant to travel long distances to such events, which have maybe become more and more like old-style 'set-piece' demonstrations: more police, more hype, more pressure to be well-prepared. Why travel 200 miles or more to demonstrate against capitalism when the capital relation is all around (and within) us? A lot of it just seemed like more work to us and when we took days off from our jobs (whether stolen or otherwise) we decided we'd rather go for picnics with our friends and children, or travel to the seaside. How could one demonstrate against a social relation anyway? And how could one describe (as many did) financial centres, such as the City of London, as being the 'heart' of capital?

These concerns fed into and were fed by an English-language debate on the nature of activism, sparked by a article, 'Give Up Activism', which was first published by RTS in their collection of *Reflections on J18*.[1] In discussions with other activists/communists/anarchists, in particular at the May Day 2000 conference, we found ourselves troubled by some of the language and assumptions of others concerning 'the movement'. We got the feeling that some felt 'the movement' constituted itself at big events like conferences, where the aim should be to discuss, agree and unite, prior to going forth into the world to spread the good word. We, on the other hand, tried to argue that (following Tronti) we have to begin with the struggle, not 'the movement', and that the movement will only come together, constitute itself through struggle.

It seemed to us that some activists saw the world in terms of us and them and them: one 'them' is the capitalists and their organisations, very clever and perhaps all-powerful. The other 'them' is 'the working class' or 'ordinary people', complicit, ignorant and/or too lethargic to 'do anything'. The 'us', on the other hand, who 'we' are, is unproblematic and well-defined: 'we' are the 'enlightened' ones. This view of the world isn't very helpful! In fact, it parallels the way the traditional left used to talk: because working-class people are not 'politicised' (or 'active'), they need to be educated and prepared for their historic role. If you're not part of the solution, you're part of the problem. Of course, this approach is mirrored in another tendency: to criticise activists mercilessly, but to see an idealised proletariat 'out there' which spontaneously makes all the 'right moves'. We ourselves have been guilty of both approaches. We see part of the struggle against capital as a struggle to dissolve this separation between 'activism' and 'life', to transcend activist/non-activist identities. [These thoughts seem very relevant to the questions on the relationships between 'activism, work and "life"' and between 'the "antagonistic movement" and other forms of "social action" and involvement'.]

These experiences, observations and debates forced us to confront what became the fundamental question for us: what is the 'anti-capitalist movement' and who is part of it? Presumably the anti-capitalist movement includes those who danced in the streets at the J18 Carnival against Capitalism in London in 1999, those who attended the May Day anti-capitalist conferences in Bradford in 1998 and London in 2000, and those who took to the streets of Genoa in 2001. The movement may also include those on the streets of Seattle in November 1999, though this demonstration was 'against globalisation' not 'against capitalism', and those who took part in various Reclaim the Streets actions in the UK, as well as those who attended either of the two *encuentros*. But would it also include, for example, those who attempted to defend Nike stores from the violence of some of the Seattle demonstrators, or those pacifists in Genoa who allegedly attacked some members of the Black Bloc with sticks? Do we count those who agreed to meet and be photographed with heads of state such as Blair or Putin? What about those who refuse to play any part in such meetings and who condemn those who do? What about those who weren't in Genoa, but who cheered the demonstrators on television? What about those who have no television?

Our ideas have also been influenced by a series of other events that have taken place in Britain over the past few years. In 2000, we saw blockades of petroleum depots by hauliers and farmers protesting increases in diesel fuel prices. The following year, we saw popular protests against paedophiles. We have also seen the growth of the far-right British National Party (BNP). All of these struggles have been far more reactionary, yet we have been as interested to understand them as the emergence of the 'anti-capitalist movements'.

The crisis sparked by the fuel protests led to a variety of interesting behaviour. Numerous people used the shortage of fuel as an excuse to avoid going to work. Others developed human relationships with their co-workers and neighbours. Shops ran out of milk and bread, yet we could see cows grazing and wheat growing in the fields: the question, why do we live like this? loomed large.

The anti-paedophile protests took an extremely reactionary form: many individuals were attacked by self-appointed lynch mobs, sometimes in cases of mistaken identity (in one case a paediatrician was threatened). Clearly, sexual abuse of children is an extreme symptom of our perverted sexuality in this society. In the here and now we have no answers to the problem of child sexual abuse and abusers, but paranoia and witch-hunts are never useful. The BNP, of course, is racist and anti-immigrant, amongst other things. In both these cases—anti-paedophile protests and fascism—the 'new possible world' which is suggested is one we would fight. In fact, their YES is a part of our NO. Yet we suspect the underlying reason for people protesting against paedophiles being housed in their neighbourhoods or for voting for the BNP is not racism or bigotry. It is instead rage against shit conditions, human needs which are not met, the disinterest and complicity of the political system, their own (apparent) powerlessness. In this respect their NO! springs from the same source as our own.

THE DOING, NOT THE BEING

In trying to make some sense of all these diverse events and struggles mentioned above, we found our conception of the 'movement' becoming ever wider, as it also became more fragmented, until it seemed to explode altogether. We are no longer sure whether it is even possible to identify any movement in the sense used in the list of questions.

We do not think we can conceive of 'the movement' as a thing, as an entity (as noun) which can be defined. Instead, we are thinking of the movement in terms of the *moving* (verb) of social relations. We are seeing examples of this everywhere

Instead of beginning with activism, we have tried to look instead at life and work in general. In particular we have tried to look at our own work and lives since these are what we have most experience of. In fact, when we started reading *Capital*, it was with the aim of trying to gain some understanding not primarily of the 'world' or the 'economy', but of the contradictory nature of our own particular circumstances. We moved from the largest determinations, the big theories of capitalism, and tried to apply them to the minutiae of our own lives. But simultaneously we moved in the other direction too, attempting to understand how the minutiae of our lives, our own actions, could affect the development of capitalism.

What is the relationship between activism, work and 'life'? This question is central since it focuses our attention on what we do. For each of us, for every single person on our planet, our life is divided into two types of doing: on the one hand, doing which is against capital (which only sometimes takes the forms of 'activism'), and on the other hand, doing which reproduces capital (work or labour). The question is complex (and 'revolution' difficult) for at least two related reasons. First, it is not always clear which type of doing is which; and second, both types of doing are frequently contained in the same activity, are intermingled.

When a 'revolutionary' organisation reproduces hierarchical structures or when being an 'activist' becomes like a job, capital—which is, after all, about the ceaseless imposition of work—is reproduced. But, when we use work-time to pursue our own projects—downloading or uploading free software or music files or communist literature from/ to the internet, teaching our students about Marx rather than neoclassical economics and refusing to grade them—then capital is not reproduced and its whole existence is threatened.

But, for all the time we manage to steal from our bosses whilst 'at work', we frequently find ourselves thinking about work projects, that is, working, in our 'free time'. And we have also found ourselves using at work skills learned through political activity: skills of chairing meetings, designing documents, public speaking and so on.

We provide other unwaged labour for capital too. Housework, schoolwork, etc., have long been recognised as work for capital. Now we are also forced to spend time on the telephone—much of it twiddling our thumbs in telephone queues—sorting out bills and trying to get better deals on utilities, mortgages, etc. This is just more unpaid labour, helping produce the use-value for capital of more competitive markets. In fact, many communists have become interested in call-centre workers and their conditions. But those proletarians who have to call the call centres provide at least as much labour for capital, all of it unpaid.

We created the world we now live in. The blurring of work and non-work is part of capital's response to our struggles of the 1960s and '70s, our attempts to flee from domination and oppression in the factory, in fields and offices, in the home, in schools and universities. As capital pursued us out of these traditional workplaces, it has been forced to adopt guerrilla tactics, to encircle us, to try and recuperate all of our activity. But as capital struggles to reduce all human activity to abstract labour, the spaces in which it is contested simultaneously expand. As Negri has written, 'the proletariat is everywhere, just as the boss is.'[2]

Only a tiny proportion of this against-and-beyond-capital doing is consciously anti-capitalist or revolutionary, and 'we'—activists, revolutionaries, communists—certainly rarely recognise it. Yet it exists in and emerges from every crevice of social life, though often in confused ways. Every day, people volunteer (gift) their time (according to their ability) to help others according to their needs. Think of people helping a parent, who may be a stranger, search for their missing child. This behaviour is human behaviour and these people begin to create human relationships, unmediated by the value relation. Reflect again on this example. It's so easy to say, 'yes but…' It's true, sometimes the media pick up on particular incidents and encourage public involvement in order to sell newspapers. But they happen every day, everywhere, human beings organise themselves according to ability and need, the child is found unharmed and nothing is reported. 'Yes, but…, it's not political'. Think again. Perhaps the problem is 'politics'.

We see the struggle between capital and against-and-beyond capital in the most unlikely places. Post-September 11, 'the world will never be the same again'. But, commercial interests (the New York Port Authority and the Lower Manhattan Development Corporation) are already gearing up to fight families and lovers of those who died in the World Trade Center over the redevelopment of Ground Zero. Most would probably not recognise it, but those who wish to ban any building on the site (a majority of those who've gone to meetings on the redevelopment plans) are fighting capital. Their doing is a doing against capital and in this sense is part of the anti-capitalist movement.

We recently bumped into an old anarchist comrade. He wasn't currently 'doing anything political', yet working as a school librarian he was making sure progressive books (for want of a better term) were stocked and he was spending a lot of time discussing issues such as the 'war on terror' with his school's students. Not 'political'? Perhaps the problem is our understanding of what is and is not 'political'. Or again, perhaps the problem is 'politics'.

CONCLUSION

How does all this relate to the 'open letter' and list of problems? We're not quite sure. Perhaps, as we suggested above, our thoughts relate only tangentially to the letter and the problems, in that we find their frame of reference problematic. In particular, we are concerned by the focus on 'activism' and by the treatment of 'movements' as thing-like, as entities, as potentially definable.

By thinking about movement(s) in these terms, we end up privileging those groups which have been identified in advance as 'political formulations' and fail to see the ways in which the majority of the world's population—'activists' and 'non-activists'—exists both within and against capital. In short, whilst every individual on the planet spends some part of their life producing and reproducing capital, they each spend another part blocking capital's (re)production and attempting to transcend it—attempting to create 'new possible worlds'. Focusing upon all forms of this against-and-beyond-capital doing, we can try and understand 'movement' as the moving, the shifting or development, of social relations, as 'the real movement which abolishes the present state of things'.[3]

Just as our own thinking isn't fixed and will continue to develop, it's important not to fix a definition on the movement. And just as our struggle is a struggle to throw off and transcend our status or identities as 'worker', 'peasant', 'housewife', 'student' or whatever, we think it important to reject and transcend our identities as 'activist' or 'nonactivist'. In fact, we think the anti-capitalist movement is a movement against identification, a movement against definition.

Moments of excess

We want to talk about 'moments of excess'. We think this idea is timely because the tactics of militant protest have recently spread to the Countryside Alliance and Fathers 4 Justice, and this can make it seem as if the direct action movement of the 1990s and the anti-globalisation movement of the 21st century have been usurped or hijacked. By considering moments of excess we can see that, perhaps, what's really happened is that our global anti-capitalist movement has kept its participants one step ahead. These days we are no longer satisfied with symbolic protest—which can almost be seen as militant lobbying. Our movement is leaning towards a more constitutive politics. People are beginning to work out what they want, what they are for, not only what they are against. What is more, people are actually 'acting' for what they want: practice not just theory. Realising that 'we live in a world of our own making' and attempting to consciously (re)make it.

Since timing is everything, we think it might be useful to look at previous constitutive moments. Moments when similar questions have been raised. We call these 'moments of excess' to emphasise what these disparate times have in common: a collective creativity that threatens to blow open the doors of their societies. The ideas we discuss are relevant to activities we are and have been involved in, such as the series of European Social Forums, anti-G8 protests and, more locally, plans for a social centre in Leeds.

∂∾

The phrase 'moments of excess' helps us make the connections between exceptional moments and everyday life. Work in a capitalist society automatically carries an element of excess because it is ultimately based on co-operation that can never be reducible to capital. Our abstract potential always exceeds and tries to escape the conditions of its production (that is, the capital relation). That's why we think there's 'life despite capitalism'; because as a living, breathing mass, our needs, our desires, our lives constantly transcend the limits of capital.

What do we mean when we say 'limits'? Capital needs to make a profit and to do this it needs to impose measure upon our activities, cramping our creativity. For example, most of us in work have some job description, however vague, laid down by management. Yet if we restrict our workplace activities to those duties, nothing meaningful would ever get done; which is why a 'work-to-rule' can be so successful. Similarly, capital needs to codify everyday practice into laws which relate to sovereign, rights-bearing individuals, even though this contradicts the way that innovation actually occurs. In fact capitalist culture tends to reduce all collective products of creativity to the sole property of individuals. 'Brunel built this…', 'Farraday discovered that…' On top of all this we have to factor in our everyday (partly unconscious) refusal to be homogenised, flattened, measured or made quantifiable.

In the most obvious sense then, there is an excess of life. In work, at home, on the bus, we produce a surplus of collectivity. This is our humanity, and it is this which capital is constantly trying to appropriate, harness, regulate or contain. All this has become more obvious over the last half-century, as capital—capitalist social relations—seems to have leaked into every aspect of our lives. At the same time, and of course related to capital's colonisation, work—our daily activities—has become ever-more socialised. It's no longer just a matter of the extraction of surplus value in the workplace: capitalist production is now inserting itself deep into the texture of our day-to-day social existence, in such a way that it now makes sense to think that society itself functions as a factory. But this increasing socialisation of labour has opened up new possibilities for co-operative and creative collectivities within capitalism that seem to lead beyond it. As work spreads throughout life so does the co-operation it relies on and it is this excess of co-operation which makes transformation possible.

∂∿

This leads us to the second, more profound type of excess. Every now and then, in all sorts of different social arenas, we can see moments of obvious collective creation, where our 'excess of life' explodes. In these moments of excess, everything appears to be up for grabs and time and creativity accelerates. From our own lives, we're thinking of punk in the mid to late 1970s, and the struggle against the poll tax in the late 1980s/early '90s, and the recent moments within the anti-globalisation movement.[1] At these times, which may have spanned several years or literally a few moments, we have glimpsed whole new worlds. But we could also mention the 1960s underground, the free software community, the popular uprising in Argentina. All of these examples are specific to a certain time and place, but we can see a common thread: a collective, liberating creativity that delights in mixing things up and smashing through all barriers. And they constantly lead back to the fundamental questions: 'What sort of lives do we want to lead? What sort of world do we want to live in?' We don't mean this in a utopian sense. Moments of excess aren't concerned with developing ideal types or blueprints of how life should be lived. Instead they deal with the possible, and represent practical experiments in new forms of life.

In these spaces, there is a real sense of subversive energy, freedom and possibility. After Seattle we started talking about 'fast-track revolutionaries'—the way that social struggles today appear to go directly and immediately to the heart of capital and its state: you can be reading Naomi Klein on Monday morning and hurling bricks at the police by Wednesday afternoon.

Perhaps the existence of 'fast tracks' is one of the defining features of all moments of excess. The concept of a 'fast track', though, is in itself too simplistic. It suggests a predetermined linear progression. Rather, moments of excess are points when time is compressed whilst the possibilities expand almost infinitely. These points are characterised by a breakdown in accepted theories and the 'laws' of capital or of political economy. In other words, 'normal' conceptions regarding what is possible in a given time and space are turned upside down. One question rapidly leads to another and the whole relation between capital and life is brought into sharp relief.

The recent anti-war movement contained moments of excess. We saw people demonstrating who'd not been on a demonstration in decades, if ever. Across the UK schoolkids walked out of classes because they heard that 'something' was happening' in town. (Often, nothing was happening... until they turned up and started something!) These people were exposed to new experiences and brought new skills and attitudes, in particular a 'do what we want' mentality. They carried no baggage regarding 'what happens' on a demonstration and this frequently made such demos difficult to police (for both paid cops and organisers) because the new protesters had little knowledge of and respect for the 'rules'. As a result new subjectivities were produced.

Another defining characteristic of moments of excess is that existing methods of mediating people's desires and demands fail. People don't stop to think what's possible, what's realistic—and no 'expert' is there to help them keep their feet on the ground. Hence the Paris 1968 slogan 'Be Realistic, Demand The Impossible'. In times of heightened activity we simply pose the only question worth asking: 'what sort of life do we want to lead?' Or even 'what does it mean to be human?'[2] And it's perhaps important to note that moments of excess are not just a modern phenomenon, they can be traced back through history. During moments of excess ('revolutionary' moments) we feel more connected to past experiments in new-world construction: to the Italian autonomists, the Naxalite rebels, the Paris Communards, the English Diggers. During bursts of revolutionary creativity we feel 'really' connected to our antecedents, not just warming ourselves with their memory.

☙

But how do these moments of excess emerge from the 'everyday' excess, our daily surplus of life? Clearly it's not a question of pushing the right buttons, or aligning the right material forces. We can't engineer these situations. But it might be revealing to turn the question on its head and look at how these moments of excess subside and return to everyday 'normality'.

Some writers have used an analogy with geological formations.[3] If moments of excess are about horizontal flows of energy and desire, there is a simultaneous pull in the opposite direction. A way of thinking about this is that possibilities are channelled in certain directions— towards static, vertical forms ('stratification' and 'striation'). One of the most exciting elements of punk, for example, was the way it broke down boundaries and identities. It was an excuse to reinvent yourself, with a new look and a new way of viewing things; this play with identity was often topped off with a new name. Other boundaries were broken by bands having shifting and multiple line-ups, or by gigs where the split between band and audience became blurred. But there was a counter-tendency, towards identification and demarcation. All of a sudden you had to wear the right 'punk' clothes, you had to know who was in the band, and the stars were always on stage.

Of course it's not as simple as saying the first was good, and the second was bad. A certain amount of stratification is necessary to focus our co-operation and energy; without it the result would be entropy—

the dispersal of energy. Stratification can have productive and restrictive moments. For instance, the way people look, talk, and hold their bodies can reflect a certain commonality and can help spread recognition of a shared antagonism. Moments of excess often produce their own common styles and common conducts. Our struggles aren't just struggles for bread and potatoes, but for new ways of being and the revolutionary movements with the most resonance (the Black Panthers, Zapatistas, etc.) have understood this. Over time such styles and the attitudes they reflect can become rigid and begin to act as a conservative force. But just as you can still see the original lava flows in rock formations, traces of the moment of excess are always present and can always be 're-activated'. That's why many of the people who threw themselves headfirst into the early days of punk were people who'd lived through those moments in the late 1960s. And why so many who became involved in rave were old punks.

Stratification also occurs as a result of attempts to defend moments of excess. In the free software movement, for example, hackers have adopted a legal framework (the GNU General Public License) in order to safeguard open-source code. They have tried to use copyright laws to lock software into communal ownership. This can be seen as a productive moment of stratification as it opens up a field of possibilities for co-operative production. However there is a danger that this could draw the free software movement towards legalistic ways of thinking. A more worrying tendency within software, and another example of stratification, is that towards homogenisation. Free software frequently mimics proprietary packages. For example Open Office, which runs on Linux, is an almost exact clone of the Microsoft Office suite of programs. But such software, although it may threaten Microsoft's profits, provides little in the way of real alternatives. These software projects 'may have freedom in the sense of free speech, but this speech is not the result of free thought. Their composition is determined by the submissive relation to the standards set by Microsoft. This is a deliberate abdication of the imagination.'[4]

In political movements, stratification often appears as a turn to 'ghetto politics', where 'purity' is the driving principle. We lived through the anarcho-punk movement of the 1980s and it's a prime example (although by no means the only one). Capital was seen as an outside 'alien' force, rather than something that is inherent in all social relations. The 'ghetto' offered the illusion of solid foundations on which we could stand and cast judgement on other efforts to escape this world.

As anarcho-punk collapsed and Class War (the organisation) grew, this grouping shifted from being a chaotic and uncontrollable force to one that was, on occasions, paralysed by its own over-organisation, bureaucracy and fear of losing itself.[5] There was a clear attempt to formalise and capture flows of energy, but it was done by defining boundaries and drawing lines in the sand which had the opposite effect from that intended. In fact, we witnessed a bizarre reversal in the 1990s, where much of our workplace life took on many of the traditional features of political action—communication, teamwork, independent and critical thinking directed towards common purpose. At the same time, 'politics' became more and more like work: a focus on 'efficiency', micromanagement, directing of resources, performance targets, and so on. To put it another way, so much of 'politics' represents the very opposite of those moments of excess: space is compressed, while time expands infinitely (who's never looked at their watch in a political meeting?).

This blinkered vision can also be seen in the holy grail of purity, beloved of many anarchists. There is an idea that one can be 'pure' in one's politics. For example, one shouldn't rent a building for a social centre—the only acceptable option is squatting. Of course, few, if any, of those arguing this position actually live in squats. Many have jobs and most make rent or mortgage payments, but this attitude derives from the misconception that 'politics' is somehow purer and separate from 'everyday' life.

We can even point to the contradictory tendencies at work in the European Social Forum. During the organising process the 'horizontals' have fought the 'verticals' to keep things open. In the process, however, people have come to define themselves as one or the other. In the past our strength has been our ability to be more than the definitions that are thrust upon us.

⊘&

One way to think this through is to make a three-way distinction between majority, minority and minoritarian.[6] In 1976 punk was minoritarian, it was undefined and open, it revealed a huge range of possibilities. But that initial urge to change, which was a process, got solidified into a never-changing state of being; a quarter-century on punk is an established minority identity. It's fine to be a punk, it poses no threat: you wear the right clothes, you mess up your hair a certain way, you listen to certain records. Capital can incorporate any identity because you aren't actually required to believe in anything for capitalism to function.

Another way of understanding the links between identity, individuality and collectivity is to look at riots. A common police strategy during big demonstrations is to (attempt to) create panic, by charging with horses, by driving vehicles into the crowd at high speed, by firing bullets (usually 'only' plastic in the North, frequently live bullets in the global South), in order to shock participants into an individual identity. Literally, 'shock tactics' whose aim is to disorient and then divide. The collective dissolves into competing individuals, all desperate for the quickest route to safety. A similar process can be seen in the days after such an event. For instance, following the Trafalgar Square Poll Tax riot of 1990, newspapers published pages of photographs of individual 'rioters': their aim to isolate through identification.

Still, it's important to note that when the police break up riots, they're not attempting to destroy collective organisation, *per se*. Rather, their aim is to re-order our collectivity in a way that doesn't challenge the capital relation—we're expected to go home and consume, to work, to reproduce. It's a high risk strategy that's only used as a last resort: driving vans into a crowd will decompose our collectivity but there's no guarantee that it will be regrouped in a way that works for capital. Stronger and/or more numerous anti-capitalist subjectivities may just as easily be the outcome.

For example, at last year's G8 summit in Evian, we experienced two different responses to police tactics. A road blockade out in the countryside (at Saint-Cergues, on the road between Annemasse and Evian) involved several hundred *disobbedienti* and other 'activists' (for want of a better word). Despite hours of bombardment by tear gas, pepper spay and concussion grenades, our self-organisation and collectivity were too strong to be broken. For us, the experience felt liberating: we participated in 'spokes-councils' for the first time, we observed a fluidity of roles and almost complete absence of demarcation of militancy; we had great fun for many reasons (which included enjoying the sun and great views of the Swiss mountains). But in some ways the action was something of a 'set-piece'. Our subjectivities against-and-beyond capital were certainly strengthened, but not fundamentally altered. (Perhaps the most interesting interactions in this respect were those between blockaders and the sympathetic residents of Saint-Cergues, who brought coffee, food, biscuits and who opened up their houses so that people could collect water, wash off tear gas, use the toilet, etc.)

The following day in the centre of Geneva, outcomes seemed much more open, more unpredictable. Following police actions to intimidate and corral demonstrators, they themselves came under pressure from outside of their cordon and found themselves surrounded. As night fell, this crowd outside became more chaotic and more menacing and the police were forced to turn their water cannon around to confront the crowd they'd created. In this urban setting, where troublemakers freely mingled with commuters, our collectivity was much weaker. On the one hand, it was easier for the police to disperse us with water cannon and plastic bullets, to push us out of the city, even if that meant moving trouble elsewhere. But, on the other hand, their actions also forced 'activists', angry but 'apolitical' youth, 'respectable' Genovese citizens into close proximity. In effect, city-centre Geneva that night became a cauldron of new subjectivities.

Yet again, we're not suggesting one situation is better than the other. In a sense, we need both. We do need to resist definition, to constantly challenge the limits they imply. But at the same time, having boundaries or identities can sometimes work in our favour, opening up other spaces for us to move into.

If shock tactics represent an excessive response to our excess, they're not restricted to riot settings. We can see the same criminalisation and demonisation at work against the free software communities. The US government is keen to claim that ripped-off corporate logos might be raising funds for terrorists. In 2001 Assistant US Attorney warned of the dangers surrounding DeCSS utility, a program which allows PCs running on Linux to read digital video disks, likening DeCSS to tools useful to terrorists, such as 'software programs that shut down navigational programs in airplanes or smoke detectors in hotels... That software creates a very real possibility of harm. That is precisely what is at stake here.'

℺

It's easy to dismiss all of this as ephemeral, to do with 'superstructure', 'culture' or 'ideology', and thus far removed from the real forces in society. Or, in a different language, to criticise it for being just about subjectivities and not about objective conditions. You might think that by talking of moments of excess we're mixing together things that are actually different; that political revolts matter and cultural revolts don't. We reject all that. Capital is engaged in an attempt to appropriate our very capacity to be human: whether we're call centre workers, office cleaners, migrants or programmers, whether we're at work or at home, what is increasingly being exploited is our very capacity to interact, to communicate, to create, to be human. By subsuming the whole of life itself, production has effectively destroyed the division between 'inside' and 'outside'. There is nowhere that is not simultaneously capital, so it makes no sense to talk of 'politics' or 'economics' or 'culture' as discrete areas.

This clearly has important implications for our idea of 'revolution'. It's usually been understood as an 'event': the execution of Charles I, the storming of the Bastille or the Winter Palace, the election of Mandela and the ANC. As a consequence, many concerns are deferred: 'wait until after the revolution...' The period 'after the revolution' then assumes the status of 'heaven' in orthodox religious thought (whether of Christian, Islamic or Jewish variety). Be good, know your place, conform, suffer, make sacrifices and wait for your (eternal) reward in the afterlife. This is exactly the language used by many revolutionaries. We are expected to suppress our own desires for the 'greater good' (of 'the people', 'the working class', 'womankind', whatever). We reject this notion of revolution and the behaviour it encourages. We much prefer Digger Gerard Winstanley's idea of a Republic of Heaven: heaven exists here on earth, we have only to create it!

But from another perspective, we are forced to ask 'Where is the rupture?' If all forms of action are socially productive, and if capital is amoral and infinitely malleable, isn't our resistance simply the creative cutting edge of capital? Will we turn round in ten years time to find that the things we're fighting for now appear against us? Will we close down Starbucks only to find a chain of organic fair-trade coffee houses clogging up our cities? Are we stuck in an eternal return where all struggles are recuperated? Do we have to give up millenarian fantasies of a mighty day of reckoning where the truth will out and the unjust shall be judged? We don't know. With no inside and outside, there is no solid foundation on which we can stand to make those judgements: all we know is that nothing is certain. Perhaps we won't even recognise rupture until after it has happened, especially if we're still looking for a winter palace to storm. In any case, 'recuperation' is itself a problematic concept, as it still works with an inside/outside logic, as if there is some place that capital can not penetrate: we'd rather think in terms of striation, where flows of energy are temporarily captured but always have the potential to 'unfreeze' and move again. This moves the problem from protecting pure spaces to keeping spaces open to the dynamism of new movements.

So what can we do to extend and expand these moments of excess? There is a general conflict between, on the one hand, our collective productivity and the creative production of our subjectivity and, on the other, capital's attempt to dampen all of this and reduce it to the valorisation of capital. At certain crucial moments, a surplus of collectivity in one sector amplifies, and ripples right through a social formation. Why? The key seems to be resonance, the way that things 'make sense' at certain points in history. Seattle made sense to millions of us five years ago: time shrank and our horizons exploded so that everything seemed possible. We can't repeat Seattle, in the same way that we can't do punk again. But what we can do is keep on the same line of opening ourselves up, constantly turning outwards rather than in on ourselves. We need to keep open not only our ways of thinking, but also the related methods of organising, the tactics, techniques and technologies we use—it's a constant battle to ward off institutionalisation. That sense of openness and movement seems fundamental to a different way of life.

Summits and plateaus

When the powerful meet, we meet. When the leaders of the world's richest nations, largest corporations, most important institutions gather to make decisions on how power will be administered, we, the **MOTLEY**, the rabble, the troublemakers, the ne'er-do-wells—the multitude—gather to exercise power.

Summits are our summits! What happens at them? On the face of it, they're about protesting, about being against things. But in fact what we do is far more positive: we spend time together, we demonstrate together, maybe riot a little; we talk together, we argue together; we dance together, we drink together, some lucky ones even fall in love... In short we **LIVE**! And we **CHANGE**: we don't come out of it the same as we went in. All of this organised in non-hierarchical, non-authoritarian ways. Frequently messy, rarely 'perfect' or 'pure', but usually in such a way as to give all of us realistic hopes of doing it better next time.

And what of before? Organising mobilisations against, say, the Group of Eight (G8) summit is an immense amount of work, involving perhaps several hundred people doing stuff up to two years in advance—with obviously many, many more people as the date approaches and far, far fewer for most of the months before that. An enormous amount of work: media stuff, networking stuff, legal stuff, health, accommodation, liaising with NGOs, trade unions, political factions, local government... and all of this co-ordinated and done with no leaders, no one telling others what to do. And, again, frequently **MESSY**??

Journalists, leftists, politicians frequently ask, 'Okay, so you're against the G8 [or the World Bank, or the...]. But what are you for?'

What an absurd question! **WE ARE FOR THIS**! This openness, this way of organising, this way of living, of being, of producing life! When we look at it like this, it's not about how to fuck them up, it's not about how much damage we can cause. It's not about them; it's about **US**. Of course it's easy to see why we keep getting dragged back on to this territory. Our summits take place in opposition to theirs, so we always end up talking about the G8, the World Bank, the IMF, the WTO, etc. But the reality is that Blair, Bush and Berlusconi meet and talk all the time. They have computers and telephones. They don't have to meet at G8 summits. So whether or not we prevent them from meeting doesn't really affect their power to make decisions. But our effect on their ability to meet is an index of the 'other worlds' we are living. It is almost a measure of their **POSSIBILITY**. Our summits and our movements aren't about destroying capitalism by fucking things up; they're about **EXPANDING** our own possibilities, turning ever outwards—**EXCAVATING** capital's power to make its world pointless.

Over the last few years the period following summits has seemed, almost by definition, one of decline. Our sense can be one of deflation, of 'coming back to earth', of returning to the world we had (fleetingly) left. Our normal world seems hollow, our jobs seem pointless. This is hardly surprising because we feel—we are!—irrevocably changed by those collective moments of **INTENSITY** and **CREATION**. The problem is how this energy, these moments of excess, can be sustained. This is nothing to do with maintaining summit links, preparing for 'the next one', keeping in touch, or anything like that. Every meeting or gathering seems to end with someone (or all of us) suggesting yet another mailing list to 'continue the discussion'—to make our wealth-producing machine permanent—and then passing round a piece of paper to collect email addresses. We're certainly not suggesting that we shouldn't stay in touch, but human beings maintain long-lived connections in different ways—more one-to-one or small group-based, and founded on shared labour, personal attraction, simply 'clicking' with one another. When we slip back to thinking about formal lists or networks, we're making unnecessary assumptions about what 'the movement' is or should be. We revert to organisational, bureaucratic ways of thinking about ourselves as a way of trying to keep something wonderful going—when those ways of thinking are the antithesis of what that 'something' was. The movement isn't a defined collection of people, it's not a network of groups, it's not even a 'thing'—it's a process, a **BECOMING**.

Summits are singular moments, moments of excess, during which we change individually and collectively. At Gleneagles we'll produce immense **COLLECTIVE** wealth and experience new ways of being. It's this we need to keep in mind as we discuss the event and how we organise for it. New processes and possibilities will emerge and it's crucial that we don't try to close these down or jam them back into pre-conceived notions or schemes. It's vital that we allow our creativity and our energy to flow freely. It's in these circumstances that our collective intelligence can ignite to generate other worlds, that we can connect the present moment to those moments of excess yet to come. Our experiments in new ways of being are limited only by our imagination: let's keep it **OPEN**... See you at Gleneagles!

Event horizon

And what is the phantom fuzz screaming from Chicago to Berlin, from Mexico City to Paris? 'We are REAL REAL REAL!!! as this NIGHTSTICK!' as they feel, in their dim animal way, that reality is slipping away from them...

— William Burroughs, commenting on the police beating protesters at the Democratic convention, Chicago 1968[1]

DOCTOR WHO

We're used to thinking of time as a straight line. When we look back at history it seems like all past events only existed to lead us to this point. And when we think about the future we can only imagine that line continuing. The future we imagine is really only the present stretched out ahead of us. Therein lies the truism that science fiction is really always about contemporary society.

But history isn't a straight line. It moves in a series of uncontrolled breaks, jolts and ruptures. Every now and then we get events that seem to have popped out of an alternate dimension. Events that don't seem to belong to the timeline we were just on. These events carry their own timelines. When they appear, history seems to shift to accommodate them. Funny how we couldn't see it before, but now we come to look there's a line of history that seems to have existed just to lead us up to this moment. Such events also seem to carry their own alternate future. Things that seemed impossible a day or two before seem irresistible now.

These moments go down in history under a flattening name. Seattle 1999. May 1968. Kronstadt 1917. They eventually get tamed and forced into the history books but their alternate futures never totally disappear. You read about these events and you can still feel the tug of the future they thought they had. You still feel their potential welling up.

Events like Gleneagles are semi-conscious attempts to engineer such ruptures in time, attempts to shatter any orderly 'progression' of history. That's why we're here. Plus, of course, it's fun... And exciting. And a little bit scary (at times very scary). Above all, we're here because we want to be. We're not here out of any sense of duty. We're not following our 'conscience'. We're following our desire! It's at events such as Gleneagles that we feel most alive, most human—by which we mean connected to the rest of humanity. And we do mean all of humanity. Not just the folk immediately around us that we know personally, not just the thousands gathered at Gleneagles (or wherever else). And our sense of connection isn't even limited to the six billion humans currently living on the planet in our six billion different ways. At times like these we can feel connected to life in all its forms. Total connection.[2]

And, of course, not only do we feel this total connection, but now everything seems possible. Anything could happen. An infinite number of new dimensions open up. What does it feel like to be inside one of these events, to be a time traveller and leap from one time line to another? And what are these possibilities? These might seem like daft or impossible questions, but we're not the only people asking them. In fact, understanding the meaning of events like this G8 'counter-summit' is one of the most important questions to think about and organise around.

CLOSE ENCOUNTERS

It's a physical thing. The hairs on the back on your arms stand up. You get goosebumps. There's a tingling in your spine. Your heart is racing. Your eyes shine and all your senses are heightened: sights, sounds, smells are all more intense. Somebody brushes past you, skin on skin, and you feel sparks. Even the acrid rasp of tear gas at the back of your throat becomes addictive, whilst a sip of water has come from the purest mountain spring. You have an earnest conversation with the total stranger standing next to you and it feels completely normal. (Not something that happens too often in the checkout queue at the supermarket.) Everybody is more attractive. You can't stop grinning. Fuck knows what endorphins your brain's producing, but it feels great. Collectivity is visceral!

It's a little like when you fall in love with someone. There's a surplus of love that gets transferred to the whole world. Simultaneously you fall in love with the individual and the whole world. It can be like this on a 'demonstration', in a riot, in a meeting, sharing food in a collective kitchen. The sense of connection you feel with the people around you becomes a connection with the whole of nature, including other humans. And we're not using metaphors here. Love is not just love for an individual—romantic love. This sense of connectedness is, in itself, love, an immanent love for the whole world. And just as with romantic love, we not only connect with everything outside, but with everything within ourselves too. Doors open, barriers dissolve—love isn't just a feeling, it's a force. We fall in love and anything becomes possible—'Nobody knows what a body can do.'[3] In fact, we're not even sure they're 'our' bodies any more. Our own accounts of those intense moments of collectivity are much closer to 'out-of-body' experiences. As we surrender ourselves to the pull of the crowd, as we sway to its rhythms, it's harder and harder to work out where the one ends and the other begins. 'My veins don't end in me.'[4] This new-found equality and collectivity is infectious, and rips like a contagion to the core of our being: we don't feel like individuals in a crowd—we are the crowd, and the crowd is in us. It's magical.

Of course this feeling of connectedness doesn't just come from romantic love or 'political' events. You don't have to have been in a riot to know what we're talking about here. The same affect lies behind religious experiences, gigs, sharing drugs, football matches and loads of other social gatherings. What's perhaps different is the presence of transcendent elements. With a congregation, our collective love is channelled through our love of god and is mediated by the priest or imam or rabbi. Or else it's channelled through the band on stage or the team on the pitch. It's far more anchored and controlled, and unity seems to come at the expense of our difference. Whether it's The Hives working the crowd at a gig or a striker saluting the Kop, these are undeniably powerful moments—but you know from the start the direction they're heading in. There's never any real transformation. But when we enter moments without a vertical element, where the energy and desires flow sideways and everyone is a leader, then we're much closer to the old idea of communion. Then we really can walk on water.

Sadly it's not possible to live at that fever pitch forever—that level of intensity is just too demanding on our minds and bodies. One way or another we have to come back 'down to earth'. But while we never seem to achieve the future these collective moments promise, that doesn't mean that things return to normal once they're over. It's like the famous duck/rabbit image. Yes, you can see it as one or the other, but once you've shifted perspective it's impossible to revert completely to the view you had before. The come-down after these events—the 'return to reality'—can be  really jarring. After the anti-poll tax riot, J18, Evian 2003, etc., all the shit on television, in the newspapers, workplace gossip and so on just seems dead, lifeless, rather than merely intensely annoying. You'd think that we'd come 'home' more angry and frustrated than ever but it's the opposite: we no longer feel like putting our foot through the TV. What's the point? The moving images on its screen are as inanimate and soulless as the box itself. Tabloid and TV crap annoys us because it seems to have an independent life apart from us, just as other commodities appear to have independent power over us. But in these huge collective events, the mist suddenly clears and we can see things for what they are. Capital is nothing. It might look like everything, but it really is nothing.[5] It's at these events and after that we see our power: we are alive and in control. The police might be screaming 'We are REAL REAL REAL!' but it's the desperate cry of a dying ghost.

BACK TO THE FUTURE

But how did we get here? For us, at least, this way of doing 'politics'— this way of being, even this way of writing—feels very different from 'politics' in the 1980s or early 1990s. Marches weren't always boring, of course, but political positions seemed rigid. You nearly always knew where you were with people. You knew where to find the 'anarchists' and the 'socialists', the 'trade unionists' and the 'greens', the way they dressed, the way they behaved. And you knew where to put them, each in their own ideological and intellectual box.

It seems to us that this shifting nature of 'politics' is linked to the shifting nature of capitalism, the transition from 'Fordism' to 'post-Fordism'. In the 1950s and 1960s, the hegemonic form of work—the form which seemed to condition other forms—was the Fordist factory. Labour on the production line may have been dull and repetitive, but it was limited, temporally, emotionally, bodily. Clock on. Perform a prescribed range of tasks, requiring a certain range of skills. Clock off. Repeat daily five days a week, 48 weeks a year for 40 years. An (apparently) clear demarcation between these stolen hours, stolen years, and (the rest of) life-time. This organisation of work—with the 'mass worker' engaged in 'mass production'—seemed to engender a certain form of 'politics', a 'mass politics' revolving around trade unions and workers' parties, whether of the 'reformist' socialist/social-democratic or 'revolutionary' variety. Of course, most people weren't factory workers, not even in the so-called advanced capitalist countries, and for most of the world's population, work wasn't limited. But no matter: the Fordist model shaped the way of the world.

All of this changed in the 1970s as the techniques and forms of industrial production shifted towards smaller, more mobile labour units and more flexible structures of production. Information, communication and co-operation have become absolutely fundamental to social production. The trouble is these things don't stop at the factory gates— in many cases, there isn't even a factory any more. Industrial labour has clearly lost its dominant role. That's not to say that it's disappeared (it hasn't) but the leading role is now taken by what's known as 'immaterial labour'—labour that produces immaterial products, like knowledge, information, a relationship, communication or an emotional response. In fact, most of the time it feels as if it's actually our whole lives that are being put to work (although we're only getting paid for a fraction of the hours we're awake). That's why people talk about the blurring of the line between work and non-work. Whatever paid work we do, the production process increasingly draws on all our social relationships, our passions, our interests outside work. In short, capital now attempts to appropriate our very capacity to be human.

To put this another way, assembly line workers in the 1930s produced motor cars, but they also 'produced' themselves as 'workers'. A whole mass of political institutions (trade unions, social democratic parties) and tactics (strikes, sabotage, wage demands, lobbying) were built on the back of this identity. Many of these traditions still exist but their foundation has long since crumbled—when we say 'I'm a computer operator/cleaner/nurse' we're just describing where this month's pay cheque is coming from. The question 'what do you do?' is increasingly anachronistic, or else invites a kaleidoscopic response. In fact the subjectivity we produce (in and out of the workplace) has changed. The key words here are flexible, mobile and precarious. Flexible because we're expected to do a whole range of tasks within our working day (which of course never ends); mobile because we migrate from job to job; and precarious because there are precious few guarantees left.

This flexibility cuts both ways: on the one hand, even the most highly paid workers are just a few pay cheques from the prospect of destitution; but on the other hand, this new-found flexibility is the result of our actions. Fordism collapsed because workers found that they didn't want to do the same job, day in, day out, for 40 years. Maybe we didn't even want to work at all... How else can we explain this 'movement of movements', which we understand as a moving of social relations? It's exploded over the last five or six years because it resonates—it 'makes sense'. In fact, crazy as it might seem, there's not a massive distinction between those incendiary moments (like Seattle, Genoa) and the rest of our lives. In and out of work, we spend our lives communicating and producing in a way that's far more visible than it was to our forebears: the world is, more than ever, our creation. That's why engaging in this whole process, living and producing here in Gleneagles, seems so natural to us—far more natural and more realistic, in fact, than relying on Bob Geldof or Make Poverty History with their rhetoric of measured demands and long term strategies. And since we're all now encouraged to be more 'flexible'—as consumers, as employees, as parents—it's actually a lot easier to imagine a different world...

Another way of looking at this is through the move from 'opposition' to 'composition'. The Fordist model of social production threw up particular forms of organisation and resistance. On the one hand there were built-in mechanisms for collective bargaining around wage demands, job conditions, grievances and so on: movements were channelled through official and unofficial trade union structures. On the other hand, when these processes broke down, there was the option of more oppositional forms—work-to-rule, overtime bans, walk-outs, slow-downs, strikes. These forms weren't restricted to work: they flavoured almost all forms of political activity, across the board. The more reformist groups followed the first approach of negotiation and engagement, the more radical groups were more confrontational.

Fast forward to the 1990s and everything starts to change incredibly quickly. Reclaim the Streets is an excellent example of a shift towards a more compositional approach. But what do we mean by composition? Maybe it's as simple as acting as though we already exist in a different reality—we reclaim a street and recompose it according to a logic different to that of cars and capital. Without exception, every political organisation in the UK has been left flat-footed by this switch, as the dreamers out on the streets suddenly became the realists. From here on in, compositional tactics are the only ones worth having. In many ways there's nothing new about this: in 1955, in Montgomery, when Rosa Parks refused to obey a public bus driver's orders to move to the back of the bus to make extra seats for whites, she wasn't 'making a protest'. She wasn't even in 'opposition'. She was in a different reality. It's a reality that can be traced back to the Diggers and the Paris Communards. We can trace it across the world to Buenos Aires or Chiapas. It's the reality underlying the slogan 'Don't Strike, Occupy!' of May 1968 and the auto-reduction practices of 1970s Italy. And this reality re-emerges here at Gleneagles: again and again, the most productive place to start is with the question of what we want, not what we're against. And we mean 'start'—sometimes we get what we want and then we realise it isn't what we wanted after all. So we start over again.

ALTERED STATES

But if history isn't just a straight line, it's also true that we straddle many different timelines. We can think of the present as being defined by a tension between alternate futures. And big events are the moment when there's a snap or a rush forward due to a change in that tension. 'A rush and a push and the land that we stand on is ours.'[6] But this rush forwards, the Event—the moment of excess or of becoming— has a history of desires and subjectivities, which are changed by the Event. So when we're engaged in those huge collective moments, not only is it easy to feel a real physical connection to people the other side of the world, we can also feel connected to people the other side of the millennium. And these moments leave indelible traces. It only takes a second for us to flip back to that place. It might be something as direct as the whiff of tear gas, the taste of a biscuit, or something less tangible—those of us at the Annemasse blockade of the 2003 G8 summit still go weak at the knees when we hear PJ Harvey's 'Big Exit'.[7]

So is Gleneagles really going to be like May 1968? No, of course not— no event is ever like any other. But we may get echoes of this, just as we'll enjoy moments that recall the first time we fell in love or the Kronstadt uprising… In fact, it's essential that we keep receptive to all those possibilities because if we're constantly stuck in one groove, it can kill all movement. There are some groups whose reality is forever 1917: they may sell papers and recruit in 2005, but in their heads they're storming the Winter Palace. Or there are others who are stuck in the jungles of Chiapas (not the Zapatistas themselves), or stuck in the European Social Forum, or stuck with the PGA.[8]

Crucial though these times and places might be, we see them in much the same way as we see opposition—as a moment of focus, but as a jumping-off point as well, a way of channelling our energies to transport us to a different dimension. Social movements often arise in opposition to some injustice: it might be live animal exports or climate change or the outbreak of war. Opposition is a way of focusing our energies, allowing a number of people to get together and channel their flows into a concentrated point. For almost a whole year, between 2000 and 2001, summit-hopping was the name of the game: from Prague to Quebec, Gothenburg to Genoa, everywhere our rulers met, we were there to greet them.

But opposition on its own, while essential, is never enough. No matter how militant, no matter how masked-up, could we ever really close down one of their summits? Could we force McDonald's/ Starbucks/Nike out of business? More importantly, did we want to? Social movements crystallise around opposition but they rapidly create new desires, and it's this aspect which is fundamental: 'the only real revenge we can possibly have is by our own efforts bringing ourselves to happiness'.[9] The Zapatista uprising would not have resonated around the world in the way it has if it had simply stayed at the level of opposition to NAFTA. Again, the move to a more compositional approach can similarly be seen in the shifting role of convergence centres: at every major summit, we've fought back ferociously against the world that is daily imposed on us, but along the way we've also discovered new ways of doing things, invented new tactics, and found a new commonality—literally created new worlds. That's why the convergence centres have become more and more indispensable: here is where desires can exercise an almost irresistible pull on people inside and outside our movements—those desires act as amplifying chambers, unleashing huge flows of energy. Social movements are enormously productive, that's why people talk about a 'buzz'—it's the hum of life, energy and desire, a constant process of contraction and expansion as a movement breathes. Way back in 1977 why did all the super-rich like John Paul Getty suddenly want to hang out with punks? Not because it was trendy but because it created a new reality, with new desires which made previous life seem hollow and irrelevant. It's when they are creating new desires that social movements seem not only attractive but irresistible. Closer to home, Make Poverty History might operate as if it's under the leadership of Bono or the *Observer*, but its real energy and impetus comes from this movement of movements here at Gleneagles and everywhere else.

Conversely social movements can and do settle down and become calcified: desires get frozen, and the life seeps out of them. It's when you get too comfortable that problems set in. When safe spaces become completely calcified and formally or informally institutionalised, then we can talk of a ghetto. It might be a social centre with paid workers, or a summit-hopping mentality, or a music scene, it doesn't much matter. A certain way of eating, of dressing, of thinking comes to dominate and starts to freeze our desires. New orthodoxies arise, and those who can interpret them the quickest become an invisible leadership, however unintentionally.

Some of this is totally unavoidable. Just as we can't live our lives at a constant fever pitch, so social movements need to ground themselves. Maybe a certain element of contraction, of taking stock, is inevitable after a period of intense expansion—after a wild night's partying, few of us can manage without some sort of safe space to retreat to. But that doesn't mean that these refuges have to be dead or closed. They can be spaces where we can experiment with other ideas, other forms of life. In fact, without some sort of safe space it would be impossible for different velocities, different movements to compose together. A few of us have been involved in a social centre in Leeds—what's really refreshing is that we can say what we really think and do what we feel passionate about without worrying that we might be 'being unorthodox' or 'making mistakes'. This has only been possible because there is enough common impetus to keep the process going while people go off in different directions or come in from different places, moving at different speeds.

It's tempting to assume that these things are simply a matter of time—that social movements start off with opposition to some injustice, explode with desire and then gradually burn out. But that'd be to miss what's really exciting about social movements, their ability to operate on a multiplicity of levels, at different speeds and on different timelines. It makes more sense to see all these processes happening simultaneously, so that calcification is present from the outset—or more accurately, that social movements are constantly solidifying and at the same time liquefying. And sometimes we need things to get a little compacted to enable us to go spinning off again to another time and place; sometimes it's only by being in cramped situations that we can make that leap and burst through those boundaries. Perhaps a key question now is how to create spaces that provide the safety to allow further experiments without then becoming stultifying. Maybe it's a matter of teaching ourselves how to distinguish flows of energy that are productive from channels that are a dead end.

Of course, we can only think about and organise around the future that's presented by the timeline we're on at the moment. But being open—to new ideas, to new connections, new ways of acting—seems much more important than that tired old question of reform versus revolution. One of the ways to blow apart that dichotomy is to get into the habit of facing 'out' as well as facing 'in'—a kind of double-jointed action. We know that the words 'in' and 'out' are problematic, because there isn't anywhere that's really 'outside', but they seem to make some sort of sense here. What do we mean by facing in and facing out? We are constantly organising safe spaces—social centres, movements, or any other community—that allow us to experiment with excavating the power of capital. This is part of what social movements do. When these spaces turn into ghettos, it's precisely because they've stopped having a face to the outside. Rather than being doors to other worlds, they've become gated communities with limited horizons: 'safe' in the sense of 'sheltered' and 'risk-free'. The way to avoid this is to keep one face open to the outside, and to operate with a more fluid notion of boundaries. We have a greater chance of seeing our experiments trigger other events that will then knock us off course, making all our plans redundant, making our demands look ridiculously feeble. Sure, things will go wrong, unexpected outcomes will emerge, but that will only open up further possibilities. In any case, we can't ever avoid making mistakes and, in fact, social movements only work by fucking up and breaking down. All we can do is experiment with the events as they come along, look for the potential of the new desires they unleash, and allow them to develop in the most productive directions.

WAR OF THE WORLDS

One way of thinking about this is through the idea of 'precarity,' which attempts to capture the precariousness of work and life under neoliberalism and has become a new buzz-word in certain social movements over the last few years. It's easy to slip into the trap of using precarity as some kind of sociological category: so precarity comes to mean talking about migrants, or workers in fast food outlets, or the 'cognitariat', or culture workers or any number of fixed identities. Used in this way, it's as though we're trying to spot the next key area: 'This will be the next round of struggles!' 'These are the new Zapatistas!' Some of us were involved in Class War around the time of the poll tax: the Trafalgar Square riot was one of our high points, but it was followed by a strange period of casting around for the next 'poll tax', as if it was simply a matter of finding it and lighting the blue touch-paper. It was a mistake. At the time we were so fixated on the forms the anti-poll tax struggles had taken we couldn't see the potential of the new anti-roads movement and the forms it developed. We couldn't see that similar underlying processes threw up differently shaped movements that could resonate with each other. History has a great way of throwing up new struggles, and new forms, from workers' councils to social forums. And they have a habit of popping up where we least expect them. If we get stuck on the forms, and ignore the dynamic that underpins them, then our demands can easily become limits.

If we shift focus away from the forms of precarity and look at the dynamic, we get a different perspective. Precarity becomes a tool to help us see connections between apparently disparate struggles. It helps us see how ideas and tactics developed in one struggle could spread to another. But what's really powerful about the idea of precarity is that it is entirely the result of our actions. The massive wave of struggles from the 1970s onwards, especially the refusal of work, were all attempts to slip the leash of Fordist control—that's where precarity comes from. Looked at this way, precarity is not in itself a bad thing, which is why some people are trying to re-think it with the slogan 'reclaim flexibility'. And it's an even richer concept when it's expanded to include a whole series of biopolitical concerns, from climate change to border controls to the 'war on terror'. In this way precarity isn't the preserve of a particular struggle or a particular set of workers—it's far closer to a universal condition of being in this world. Our lives seem to hover permanently on the edge of an abyss as we try to pick our way through a permanent state of exception. In fact, it's increasingly become clear that all the language and technologies of securitisation—surveillance, ID cards, 'war on terror', etc.—are not intended to produce a feeling of security but rather to perpetuate insecurity. Combating this generalised insecurity can only really be done through the mobile safe spaces created by social movements.

Events such as Gleneagles are really experiments in creating new worlds. It's not that these events, these moments of excess, contain the seeds of new worlds, they are new worlds. In one sense little has changed. We are living, more or less, in the same physical bodies, the same collections of molecules. And we are not some 'marginal' segments of humanity, 'extremists' or 'politicos'. Rather, we are everyone. People who know how to heal or to grow food, people with skills in parenting or constructing physical structures, above all, people with skills in simply being human. Think what we have created here: collective kitchens, medical facilities, the 'trauma' zone[10]... It's not that this horizontal, network form of organising is more 'democratic', it's so obviously better, more 'efficient', and more 'productive'.

But wait a minute; perhaps these new worlds aren't alternate realities. As we look around we see all the parts of the previous world are still there. Except they seem rearranged slightly. Displaced just a few centimetres and yet that makes all the difference. When we're hemmed in, all the affects of precarity seem terrifying and debilitating. But as soon as things start moving, those same affects become advantageous—precarity becomes flexibility and all those attitudes and techniques we've needed just to survive suddenly become tools of liberation. It's the same as the principle of ju-jitsu: with one deft move all the multiple fears and insecurities that politicians dump on us, all the shit about immigration, terrorism, crime can be turned to our advantage. What previously seemed a cramped, crushing world full of limits and restrictions now seems a world of almost unlimited possibilities. That's the promise of the situation, that the new capacities that we feel at events like Gleneagles can be made concrete in our everyday, habitual lives. That we can develop new tactics, new technologies and new ways of living that will cause a cascade of events to sweep through society.

On the road

We all realized we were leaving confusion and nonsense behind
and performing our one and noble function of the time, *move*.
And we moved!

— Jack Kerouac, *On the Road*

It's 3am. We're midge-bitten and piss-wet through, hiding out in some
woods two miles above the A9 in Scotland. We've spent the last few
hours like extras from *The Great Escape*, stumbling through the countryside, dodging police cars and helicopters with searchlights. Now we're
trying to get a couple of hours kip in the open air, worrying about how
we're going to manage that last yomp to the road and how we're going
to block it when we get there. In the back of our minds is that conversation we had discussing the possibility that the police will send dogs
into the woods to flush us out. We're tired, hungry, and nervous. One
of us starts to giggle. It's infectious. Before long we're all shaking hys-
terically, cracking up at the sheer insanity of the situation. 'What the
fuck are we doing? How did we get here? This is madness!'

It's what alcoholics call 'a moment of clarity'. After being caught up
in the logic of the situation you get a flash of objectivity and a sense
of its ridiculousness. Hang on a minute, perhaps we ought to reverse
that. Capitalism is organised in an entirely rational way. The only irra-
tional thing about it is the whole thing: capital itself, which exists only
to increase its own value. The bottom line for the whole system is the
expansion of zeros on an accounting sheet. From that point of madness a delirium sweeps through the whole of society making our lives

seem out of control. Just as a sailor who returns from months at sea can feel dry land swaying, it's capital's delirium that you perceive in a moment of clarity. It's not us that's insane. In fact we, our movement, are the realists. Of all the organisations, groups and actors circulating around the G8 summit, we were the only honest ones. We were the only ones not offering pie-in-the-sky solutions it's obvious wouldn't be tried and wouldn't work anyway. The only ones not asking our 'leaders' to do things we know they can't and won't. Anything we want to happen we do ourselves, here and now. You end up in some mad situations when you try and act sane in an insane world but it's a different kind of delirium we're after.

☙

It's the intensity of it that makes you feel so alive. In the Hori-Zone, in the couple of days running up to the blockades, everywhere you looked there were groups of people gathered in intense and passionate discussion. Talking, thinking, planning, arguing, agreeing, co-operating. Intense communication permeated the whole camp like an electric charge. It comes from that realisation that no one's in charge, that there's no secret committee with a secret plan who are going to come and save us. If this summit is going to be blockaded it's down to us, collectively. We were all moving so fast. One evening we emerged from one meeting at 11.30 and realised we needed to rush to grab something to eat as we had to be at another in half an hour. Who on earth arranges meetings at midnight? We had to, time was tight. It all made perfect sense. Meetings are normally painful exercises in frustration, but here it was different. There was such an intense concentration of effort, such focus, that creativity, wit, imagination, flexibility and good sense seemed to come naturally. You could stagger out of a meeting drunk on the sense of connection with the other people. Vibrating with it. It was that visceral. Then, on the Wednesday of the blockades, in the fields next to the road that intensity was ten-fold. Decisions were made so quickly you barely had time to think. Look! that lot in the next field are trying to get on the road, the police are going to block them. Let's charge down here and draw the police off. Great idea, I'll join in. Next time, hey, the police aren't falling for it. They don't believe our fake charges any more. That means we're unopposed. Here we go. Over the fence. On the road. Block the traffic. Yeh, this is actually working. We're running rings around them. We're too smart for them. We're thinking too fast.

Of course it wasn't all like that. There are different speeds to decision-making and for a long time the Dissent! network moved slowly.

There are times when we need to pick things apart, think critically about the aims of what we're doing. Prise out the underlying assumptions of the way we see things. This tortoise work is what makes it possible for us to go light-speed when we need to. Similarly it's important not to elevate openness into some abstract principle. Openness on its own is not an answer. At Gleneagles, we were alive to all possibilities, but only as long as they were aimed at shutting down the summit. In fact, there had been a debate about whether we should even go to Scotland at all: if capitalism is global and ongoing, shouldn't we just attack it everywhere and every day? Wouldn't decentralised actions all over the UK avoid the concentrations of police? These critiques miss the point that capitalist summits such as Gleneagles (or Seattle or Genoa or Evian) can also be moments of concentration for us, where we can feel our collective strength and achieve together things that we can't achieve apart. Once we had decided to go to Scotland and disrupt the summit we were able to be more open about how people did that. It's similar to how open source software licences allow others to remix and build upon your work, as long as they license their new creations under the same terms: on the road blockades people could come and be as 'militant' or as 'fluffy' as they liked, as long as they didn't restrict the ability of others to do the same. With that focus, we had a commonality that allowed diversity. It was a moment of productive stratification, of closing down some possibilities in order to open up others.

After that virtually every other organisational move helped to keep options open. Everything we organised in advance was about creating the preconditions of spontaneity. We organised the infrastructure to allow people to be in the right areas with the space and time to organise themselves to do what they wanted. At the Hori-Zone, in meeting after meeting we made decisions to defer final decisions, or rather, we made decisions that maximised our degrees of freedom. Our bottom line seemed to be: how do we keep things open? It would have been easy to go for a single set-piece battle in an attempt to shut down the summit. But that would have flattened all of our compositional efforts (creating and maintaining multiple convergence spaces, each containing a whole range of subjectivities) into one spectacular moment of opposition. Instead, we planned multiple blockades and actions wherever and however we wanted to. At a site-wide meeting on the Monday evening, we decided to focus on the blockade of the A9, rather than the M9—blockading the A9 simply provided more options for individual groups to maintain their autonomy and express their imagination and creativity.[1] And once we'd decided on the A9, some people floated the idea of crashing a car on this road as a way of initiating a blockade; but in the end that too was rejected because it would have re-introduced hierarchical coordination and a single location, moving us back from a multi-pointed attack into something more traditional and easy to control. Instead the decision was a repeat of ones we'd made in the run-up to the summit: get ourselves, our bodies, in the right general area, at the same time with useful tools and a shared affect, a group feeling of collective purpose. With those preconditions met we all had to trust that a spontaneously generated collective intelligence would ignite as groups formed, split up and re-formed in a rolling blockade that was impossible to control. When there's no conspiracy, no back-room leaders pulling our strings or marking up maps, it's up to all of us to join the dots. When this happens successfully there is immense creativity with the emergence of new and unexpected properties and capacities.

❧

This isn't a new non-linear Leninism; we're not in control. Even when all the right preconditions are in place there's no guarantee that things will gel and cohere. And even if they do there's no guarantee that what emerges will work. In fact our movement only works by fucking up, by our learning from our mistakes and daring to try new things. If we look at the movement in the UK over the past decade, there's been a pragmatic strain running through it and setting the pace. Deeply intelligent, but not hung up on ideology and led off down the many dead ends that can bring. We can chart this movement by observing it breaking the surface of visibility from one event to the next, constantly searching to move on by solving the problems thrown up by the last one. Each event opening up its own problematic. One of the issues being worked through over the last ten years or more is how can we give up activism? Or rather, how can we give up the transcendent role of the activist? How can we act without being controlling and prescriptive? When Reclaim the Streets (RTS) emerged after the anti-Criminal Justice Bill protests it was an audacious switch from opposition to composition. Instead of simply protesting against cars and capital, we recomposed reality, creating car-free common space in the here and now. We started with the question of what we're *for*, rather than what we're *against*. But RTS actions always walked a fine line between the open and the secret: street parties need a clandestine layer of organisation to ensure that the crowds, sound systems and blockading equipment arrived at the right place at the same time. One of the problems with this was that people could just passively receive these events and the experience of collective intelligence could be hard to ignite. The J18 Carnival Against Capital can be seen, among other things, as an attempt to solve this problem. The May Day Guerrilla Gardening was another attempt to solve it by making passive reception less likely, but the preconditions for spontaneous action weren't there. You need time and space to self-organise and this is the real value of convergence centres—the Hori-Zone in Stirling, the VAAAG at the Evian G8 counter-summit, the 'no borders' camps.

The state has also unwittingly accelerated this drive towards more and more horizontal forms of organising. It has acted as a hostile evolutionary environment forcing immanence—a horizontality and openness—on the movement. Communication is a good example: after the EU summit in Gothenburg in June 2001, eight people were found guilty of 'coordinating and inciting riots', and sentenced to varying terms of imprisonment, for running an info-line during the protests (they'd collected information from scouts and scanners and then used it to tell activists where they were most needed). Faced with this sort of extreme repression, there are two options. The first is to organise even more secretively, making sure, for example, that the info-line's location is known to only a handful of people and utilising a range of technologies to keep transmissions hidden. The problem with this approach is that ultimately we can never beat the state at its own game: we will always be militarily defeated. The alternative strategy is to remove any remaining layers of direction and control, and effectively create a peer-to-peer network. When we rang the info-line this year, we were told 'There have been reports that...' or 'The BBC is saying that...' The info-lines were a sounding board, bouncing facts and figures back to people in the field. Information was shared, but no one was told what to do or where to go: a critical difference. During the morning of the blockades they were a means of maintaining the collective affect when many people were physically split up and wanted reassurance that they weren't the only people about to rush onto the road.

This horizontal approach allowed diversity, flexibility and mobility to feed off each other, and this intoxicating mix was fundamental to our success. On the opening day of the summit people switched seamlessly from one tactic to another without slowing down. As we made our first foray onto the A9 a few of us immediately started assembling the makings of a barricade—a few rocks and a large plastic wheelie bin. But, outnumbered by rapidly approaching cops... *switch!*... sit down on the road and all link arms. Our action immediately becomes 'Peaceful protest! Peaceful protest!' For years, the state and media have attempted to label us as 'good' protesters or 'bad'. 'Peaceful' or 'violent'. 'Legal' or 'illegal'. Dissent! or Make Poverty History. And we've often been complicit in this process of definition. While constituted parties, organisations and their spokespeople have denounced 'violent protesters' and 'trouble-makers', militants have just as frequently revelled in their distance from more constitutional forms of protest. And the police have always used the good cop/bad cop routine as a further way to divide and confuse us. This time around, however, it was us who shifted the roles, both individually and collectively: masked-up militant; pink and fluffy fairy; obliging bystander; outraged citizen. Most of the time the police simply didn't know whether they were going to be hit with a stick or a barrage of legal jargon (or even a dollop of baby sick!); whether we'd be surly or happy to share a smile and a joke; whether we'd ask friendly questions regarding their own accommodation or mock them with kisses and feather dusters... Quite simply, for long periods we wrong-footed the state with our versatility. The advantage we have is that we're quicker to respond, more flexible and far more dynamic than they can ever be. Faced with an obstacle, we can re-route, while they have to refer to their officer in charge. Another moment sticks in our memory: two people blocking the A9 dual carriageway simply by holding up a wagon alongside a van; trapped at the back, with no room to squeeze past, the police could only rev their own minibus in frustration.

This diversity of approaches and tactics, far from making us feel weak or divided, only seemed to strengthen the incredible feeling of connection. When we heard about the successful blockade of the M9, we felt as if we had been there too (even though we were 20 miles away on the A9). When we heard that the Gleneagles fence had been breached, we felt it was us who'd torn it down. Those people who had chosen to be medics or to stay in the convergence centres and cook reported the same feelings of connection, of having done it all. Everyone felt a part of everything. Again this was one of the crucial roles of the Stirling rural convergence. There are times and places when we need to ground ourselves, to take stock, re-focus and re-connect. The Hori-Zone wasn't just a low-impact self-sufficient eco-friendly experiment. Like social centres across the world, whether permanent or temporary, it offered a base camp, a safe space to retreat to.[2] Without that common place, it would be impossible for different velocities, different movements to compose together. It allowed a space for people to go off in different directions (sometimes literally!) or come in from different places, all moving at different but consistent speeds.

Seen in this light, the whole process was a great example of collective intelligence. No single person or group had total knowledge. Instead there were countless overlapping zones of skills, experience and information, and the only entity which had the bigger picture was the living, breathing movement itself. Of course, it's a hard thing to deal with. Some people never quite cottoned on to the No Plan idea and kept on waiting for it to be 'revealed'. As late as Wednesday lunchtime, when we were still playing cat and mouse with the police on the A9, we were asked by some other protesters: 'What d'you want us to do?' All we could reply was 'Do what you want!' But the day before, on Tuesday morning, even we were starting to have doubts about the approach. We couldn't see how we could manage to get thousands of people out of the camp and into the hills. But we were asking the wrong question: as individuals, the task seemed daunting because it was hard to see the collective intelligence at work. But in a mass meeting of 300-plus, the strategy made sense because we could feel our collective power: across the site, people were already self-organising, starting to make their own plans. One of us spent several hours on Tuesday afternoon and early evening driving a minibus. No Plan. Groups simply consulted a map and worked out their own plan: 'There's 11 of us. We're planning to walk somewhere up in the hills. Can you drop us off here?' 'We're going to camp at this spot. We want you to drive us there. Can you do it?' Drivers are important, of course, but they're frequently seen as having a certain authority too. Not this time and it was fantastic.

☙

As we've already said, flexibility and a collective being don't arrive by magic. It's a question of creating the right conditions and the right space in which they can emerge. And once established, they have to be guarded and defended. There's always a temptation to revert to old, more established ways of being and doing. On the Wednesday morning we were part of a meeting on a hillside in the rain at 5.30am. As well as being nervous and wet, we were all more than a little confused. It was hard to see any collectivity emerging, even though there were at least 100 of us. A few scouts reported back and told us that a 20 minute walk would take us down to the closest section of the A9... and into the arms of the waiting police. Isolated from other groups, and not really knowing what was going on, the mood of the meeting drifted quickly towards this option. Luckily, a few people refused to accept this, and argued we should stick to the original idea, to hit the A9 at multiple points north east of the Greenloaning junction, even though it meant a much longer hike into uncertain territory. The meeting swung back again and we became a collective body, focusing instead on the practical: which road to take, how to meet up with other groups, etc. In situations like this, it takes more than confidence or bravado to make that leap of faith; we need to feel that connection with others. Solidarity. The scenario was re-played as we reached the road for the first time: faced with police screaming orders, there was a moment's hesitation before, as one body, we vaulted the barbed wire.

This connects to another point. We don't just need the space and the conditions, we need the tools. This might be something as simple as a physical infrastructure: marquees, kitchens and common meeting spaces were central to the working of the barrios in the Hori-Zone, even more so than at Evian. But we can widen the idea of tools to include the whole notion of consensus decision-making and spokescouncils. They seem to have taken root quickly but, to us at least, are still relatively new. Without them, we would have been lost. Consensus allows us to create collective bodies and establish collective intelligence. It might seem insane now, but in the space of six frantic hours on Wednesday morning we took part in at least three spokes-councils in the hills and fields around the A9, each involving more than 100 people. And each time we managed to arrive at brave and imaginative decisions. It was a way of slowing things down to reassess. Of course all constituted forms can become empty and institutionalised. What they rest on are affects held in common, the right collective feeling—which allows us to cohere, allowing the range of velocities consistent with each other to be widened.[3]

☙

Commonality is always precarious. The success of our actions in the first few days couldn't be sustained indefinitely, and the forces that worked to our advantage for the first day of the summit turned against us when news of the July 7 London bombings filtered through. In Stirling, we experienced them as a moment of vertical power which effectively demobilised many of us. Earlier in the week at the site-wide meeting to discuss strategies for the opening day, there was an amazing fluidity, and a clear willingness to engage and to find common ground. But by Thursday morning many people had reverted to a default mode of either partying or party politics: there was another massive site-wide meeting, but this time it was dominated by ideology and old-style politics.

We came up against a widespread feeling that we had to 'take a position', and there was an energy-sapping effort to draft a press release. In fact, 'taking a position' was the last thing we should have done. We should have dealt with this external event in the same way a crowd of 200 of us dealt with an oncoming police car which attempted to block our path early on Wednesday morning: we literally flowed around it. 'Taking a position' means standing still and losing the initiative. It also means that it's hard to reconcile the different speeds and directions people are travelling in. After Thursday the mood, affect, feeling, buzz— call it what you like—was defensive and closed, compared to previous days: the desire had gone, and with it the energy.

Of course, it's easy to over-state the impact or significance of the bombings. They were simply the flip-side of the liberating processes we'd enjoyed over the previous days: there's always a comedown, even though this was a particularly intense and accelerated one. When we were on the move, all the affects of precarity were exhilarating and empowering. But as soon as things stopped moving, those same affects became disadvantageous—flexibility became precariousness and all those attitudes and techniques we'd developed suddenly became obstacles to liberation. On top of that, we experienced these bombings as an entirely mediated event. The TV, radio and press had a field day, sucking everything into the black hole of endless speculation. For a time we were tempted to see the bombings as proof that there are far wider forces at work, making our mobilisations at Gleneagles and elsewhere pale into insignificance. This is the deflationary effect of all mediation. But in fact the opposite is true. Our week in Gleneagles, just like all the weeks before and since, makes it even clearer that there is no 'wider' field of play, no 'real world' outside of what we do. There is one power, and it's ours.

The whole idea of the counter-summit wasn't really about protesting against the G8. For us, it wasn't even directly about abolishing global poverty. It was about life. It was about being and becoming human. It was about our desire. No matter how 'well-paid' or 'secure' our employment, as we shuffle pieces of paper, as we gaze out of the window in a meeting, as we trudge around the supermarket, we think 'there must be more to life than this...' We never felt this in Scotland, no matter how frustrated we became in one or two meetings, however pissed off we got with a few individuals or angry at the state. This was living; this was being human. This 'ragged and ecstatic joy of pure being'.[4] Of course, it's easy to dismiss this as if it's simply about a 'feeling' or an obsession with 'process'. But doing stuff for ourselves, making decisions, running our own lives… this process of creation, invention and becoming isn't a 'feeling', it's a material reality. The new capacities we experience at these events don't just disappear. They are there to be accessed during the rest of our lives… if we can work out how to reach them again.

Fundamental change starts with small, localised, material innovations, perhaps the introduction of new tools, technologies or ways of thinking. But every now and then these incremental changes build up into an event, a moment of excess, where so much life is produced that it overflows existing social forms. We spend most of our political lives developing such tools but we never quite know when an event will arise or what the effect of it will be. Nevertheless, 'we lean forward to the next crazy venture beneath the skies.'[5]

What is a life?

Walk into a bookshop and you'll see the shelves groaning under the weight of self-help books. Pick up a newspaper and you'll be groaning under the weight of lifestyle guides. Yet every survey shows an increase in fear and a decrease in happiness. This shouldn't surprise us. Just as the avalanche of cookery programmes on TV hasn't made us cook any better or any more often, this lifestyle advice isn't meant to change our lives. Alongside food-porn, or garden-porn we get lifestyle porn.

Can you imagine self-help guides that really did aim to transform your life?

A reader writes in complaining of dissatisfaction with her relationships, the agony aunt replies: 'If you want a real insight into love you should participate in a riot.'

A lifestyle columnist writes a piece on their feelings of tiredness: 'I've found the cause, it wasn't a zinc deficiency but capital's inherent need to increase its value.'

A book of tips on how to be effective: 'Creativity happens in groups, form one and collectively create new worlds.'

Surely any honest self-help book would have to start here but it would have to end by destroying our idea of what a self is. A self-help book against the self—let's pre-order.

This idea isn't as frivolous as it sounds. The self-help industry emerged because our struggles in the 1960s and '70s destabilised the post-war institutions that used to give us a firmer sense of self. Now we no longer have a job for life or communities based around an industry. The self-help industry is there to shore us up. But it also developed out of the subjectivities thrown up by the struggles of the 1960s. Through the 1970s there was a movement away from collective experiments with anti-capitalist moments towards a concentration on the self. Anti-establishment attitudes have been eaten up by capital and used as the basis for a whole new wave of consumption and work. But we have to ask if capital has found anything indigestible in what it has swallowed. Are there traces of collective anti-capitalism that can still be re-ignited?

This urge for self-transformation is the same urge that animates social movements. All that is needed is to exceed the straitjacket that capital has imposed on it. Hidden away on the pages of the Sunday supplements, obscured by the empty sheen of the latest commodity, we can still detect the outline of moments of collective creativity when people asked such fundamental questions as: What sort of life do we want to live? Or indeed: What is a life? We want to re-insert that collectivity back into the urge for self-transformation.

In order to be happy I'll have to change the whole world!

REAL WORLD

In our lives we've all experienced moments of excess during which we feel that total connection with our fellow human beings, when everything becomes possible, when absolutely anything could happen. They might be small, almost personal moments like weddings or falling in love. They might take place around counter-summit mobilisations (like Gleneagles or Evian or Genoa). Or they might rise up over a few months (like the anti-war movement of 2003, the anti-roads movement of the late 1990s or the Argentina uprising of December 2001, or, from another time and space, punk). They are moments when our energy threatens—or rather promises—to spark a cascade of changes, which sweep through society, opening up a whole new range of possibilities. When we rupture capital's fabric of domination: breaking time. Rapture![1]

But these events—these moments of excess—can't last forever, at least not in that form. It's simply not possible for our bodies and minds to survive that level of intensity indefinitely. Part of the dream-like unreality of those moments is that we are cut loose from our normal day-to-day life (home, kids, work). At Gleneagles, for example, we could really act fast and be open to all possibilities because we were stripped bare. That's why counter-summit mobilisations are so attractive: they have the potential to catapult us into a different way of being far quicker than would be possible if we had to take all our 'baggage' with us. But it's also why the high wears off: because (all other things being equal) it's unsustainable in the face of 'normality'. When we take part in these events we often leave behind lovers and/or loved-ones behind—whether physically or mentally. We feel the tug of our allotment or garden, or maybe there's a favourite bike ride or view we need to enjoy again. 'There is a rose that I want to live for... There is a town unlike any other.'[2]

We need to understand what happens when we 'return' to the 'real world'. What role can such moments play in a life?

In these events we feel a real rush of energy, a coming-together. But afterwards how can we sustain this movement in our 'habitual lives', and avoid recriminations and a general falling-apart? After the high point of *autonomia* in Italy in 1977, thousands turned to drugs or cracked up. Not just because of State repression, but because the forms of life they had been living were no longer sustainable. The expansive experiments broke down and the collective body was dismantled, and so attempts to live this life reverted to the level of the individual where contradictions were, for many, too intense to handle. How do we avoid this? How can we 'do politics' in the 'real world'? How can we 'live a life'? Not as a question of survival—hanging on in there until the next event, or our fortnight's holiday in the sun, or our Friday-night bender, or our Sunday-afternoon walk in the park, or our 'adventure weekend'—none of which are any real escape from capitalism at all. How do we live a life despite, and against, capitalism?

There are no universal answers to these questions. But we believe that thinking about them can help us understand the potential of various issues and struggles—urban development and 'regeneration', climate change, precarity and so on—perhaps help us recognise our own power in a productive way, that is, in a way which allows it to resonate and become amplified. It can help us understand what we do in social centres, for example, and the way we conceive the borders between 'inside' and 'outside', between what is 'pure' and what is not. And it involves recognising that we always live in the real world, that there are no 'pure spaces', there is no 'pure politics', and that we should welcome this. Because purity is also sterility. It's the messiness of our 'habitual' lives which gives them their potential. This messiness, this 'impurity', the contaminations of different ideas, values and modes of being (and becoming) are the conditions which allow mutations, some of which will be productive. It's from this primordial soup of the 'real world' that new life will spring. 'Only in the real world do things happen like they do in my dreams.'[3]

SAFE EUROPEAN HOME

One of the tools we've used to think about these questions is the idea of 'safe space'. In the context of summit protests we can see the development of convergence centres as the emergence of safe spaces—temporary zones to which we can retreat after a protest, gather our thoughts and recompose ourselves before we sally forth again. Just as in breathing, they are moments of contraction, before and after expansion. The Hori-Zone at Gleneagles (the eco-village in Stirling) worked really well as an example of this, providing space for food, drink, sleep as well as consensus decision-making and a thousand fireside chats—all of which combined to allow us collectively to feel our strength and focus our energies. It's no surprise that if you look at the development of counter-summit mobilisations from Genoa through Evian to Gleneagles we see the convergence centres playing a more crucial role each time. After every moment of excess there must be a retreat back to a safe space, back to a stratified body of some kind in order to analyse and recuperate before we can launch forth on another intensive experiment. And this idea of safe space doesn't stop there. We can link it to the development of a whole network of social centres, both in the UK and across the world, which perform the same function of concentrating energy and allowing collective creativity to flourish.

But this is where things start to get complicated. At summit protests, as convergence centres have become more established, they have become more open to the criticism that they are divisive, housing 'activists' in one or two designated areas while the rest of the world passes by on the outside. Some people refused to take part in the Hori-Zone at Gleneagles for precisely this reason. While some of these criticisms are harsh (there are practical considerations here after all), it does bring us right back to fundamental ideas of the 'movement'. It's a word that gets thrown about like confetti but just what does it mean?

The most obvious way of thinking about this is to say that the movement is a collection of individuals connected by means of some shared ideology or practice—the global anti-capitalist movement is simply made up of those individuals who are consciously, collectively and actively opposed to capitalism. And it's a kind of shorthand that we all use on occasions. But it's not an idea that's particularly useful. First, what does 'active opposition' mean? Obviously it includes everyone who tried to blockade the G8 summit at Gleneagles (and partly succeeded). But would it also include everyone in the Hori-Zone, for example? And what about those who couldn't make it? Or those who would have gone if they'd known about it? Second, and more fundamentally, what about those who took part in the Make Poverty History demonstrations? Are they part of the anti-capitalist movement? Or those who went to the Live8 concerts? Or even Bob Geldof, infamous for describing many of us as 'a bunch of losers'? Just where do we draw the line?

Maybe drawing the line is the problem. If we simply expand the definition of movement, we're still limited by the fact that we're thinking of movement as 'a thing'. It is something that can be defined, whose boundaries can be clearly mapped, and which stands outside and against something else called 'capital'. We might argue over the exact terms of the definition (do we include Make Poverty History or Globalise Resistance?) and we may agree that these definitions will shift but this movement is still seen as a 'thing'. But it's difficult to reconcile such a static, 'thing-like' view of the anti-capitalist movement with the realities of everyday life where the vast majority of us around the world exist both *within* and *against* capital. 'Capital' is not something 'out there', something that we can fight against as if it were external to us and part of someone or something else—even if we sometimes talk about it as if it is. 'Capital' is not a person or group of people, nor an organisation or group of organisations. Capital is a social relation mediated through commodities. Capital is the way we live, the way we reproduce ourselves and our world—the entire organisation of the 'present state of things' as they are today.

So, if there is a line, then it's a line which runs through each and every one of us. And that's why capital fucks us up—because everyone of us is fragmented, contradictory. Or if there is a line, it's fractal, with sometimes only a hair's breadth separating the 'revolutionary' from the 'capitalist'. Or maybe rather than drawing lines to say who is and is not in this thing called movement, we'd be better off drawing lines like projected or potential routes to follow—directions, deviations, lines of flight. Not where we are, but where we're *going*. It is human practice— what we *do*—which is central, because capital is the way we live, the way we reproduce ourselves and our world. So we're all always already moving, even when we think we're standing still. And we're moving along several lines and through several planes at once.

To put it another way, if we begin with the doing, then 'movement' is a dynamic process, one that resists definition. So our movement is a historical phenomenon, not a 'structure', nor even a 'category', but something which *happens*.[4] Movements are the moving of these social relations of struggle—in crude terms, movements not of people, but of people doing things in a particular time and space. A series of contractions and expansions, as social relations move through moments of excess. And this matches our own experiences: we've never come out of these moments the same as we've gone in. Whether at Evian or Gleneagles, we've come out as different people.

> The road to the station is blocked by a line of CRS police vans, in front of which is a small pro-CPE demo of about 10–15 people, in front of them there's a line of CRS on foot, and in front of them a double line of demonstration stewards preventing a confrontation. Most of the demonstrators are not up for a confrontation, but some chuck eggs, cans, fairly light things at the pro-CPE demo. The stewards, who are mainly students, are urging demonstrators to continue quickly past—they're really enthusiastic about giving orders. Someone ironically shouts, 'Be submissive! Do as you're told!' One of the stewards I know personally—he's the son of anarchist friends: I shout angrily at him, 'Have you got no shame? How can you protect your enemies?' He looks upset. *Lycée* and technical college students hold a sit-down meeting in the big square in the centre of town, lots of different youths getting up to speak, though nothing beyond youth precarity is talked about. A cry goes out— 'To the station!', echoed by a 16 year old girl from my village, who says she wants to occupy the railway tracks. Having given her a few English lessons a year or so before, I had no idea she was rebellious. Funny how you don't know people until there's a situation like this—and perhaps people don't really begin to know themselves until there's a situation like this... People return to the main square, where already people are drifting off towards the Corum Theatre in order to occupy it. Some think the call to go to the station was a manipulation so as to have time for the cops to get to the Corum... I see the guy I knew who'd been a demo steward protecting the pro-CPE demonstrators three hours earlier, the son of anarchist friends, and he waves me over, saying, 'What I did earlier back there was stupid, really stupid, but I was the first to get truncheoned by the cops here, trying to get into the Corum.' If I was religious, I'd call it 'redemption', but let's just call it 'radicalisation': sometimes radicalisation only takes a few hours.[5]

Looking at things this way round gives us a fresh perspective on safe spaces and the way different ideas of movement fit into them. One of the common ways of looking at social centres is to think of them as static safe places that incorporate a number of people, and so by definition exclude others. So we often talk about them in terms of exemplary practice: 'This is a model of how the world could be run, without bosses, without money, without hierarchy, without milk...' This notion also underpinned much of the Hori-Zone at Gleneagles. But models only work when all the actors within them know their lines. They are tightly scripted performances, with an inside (the activists) and an outside (variously described as 'consumers', 'ordinary folk' and even 'people who've not had the benefit of a university education'). It's not that far removed from the traditional Leninist view of a disciplined cadre who organise the rest of us. And in fact that inside/outside distinction gets taken even further as we start to look for points of intervention in the 'outside' world. 'Precarious workers, asylum seekers, Zapatistas—there's a whole world of struggles out there we should be engaging with...'—as if these struggles are already separate from us.

Obviously at times it's useful to draw lines. Sometimes it's even essential. When we were setting up a social centre in Leeds, it felt like there was a lot at stake (we were in a 'precarious' situation where decisions carried real weight), so destructive influences had to be confronted and contained before they jeopardised the project. Boundaries were set and one person physically expelled. But this was also productive, allowing people who had never worked together to immediately find common ground. Sometimes that sort of cramped space can itself generate intense creativity, as we fight to overcome the limits we have set ourselves. In this case, it enabled us to hold one of our most exciting and expansive meetings where people outlined what they wanted in a social centre, irrespective of cost or practicality (we never did manage to get the 50 metre swimming pool...).

All the same, if movements are a moving of social relations, it doesn't make sense to talk of static boundaries or limits: 'These people are involved at the social centre, and these people aren't...' Instead of looking at social centres as models from which we can to try and establish some sort of hegemony, it might be more fruitful to think of them as *experiments*, ones that by their very nature over-run boundaries and definition. To take one example: why do many social centres take it as axiomatic that they should open a cafe? If we think of centres as models, then a cafe can instantly offer a more environmentally sound lifestyle, living proof that we don't have to fuck over the planet to survive. But if we think of them as experiments, as attempts to create multiple new worlds, then a cafe is not an end in itself, it's a precondition—a way of getting people into a building and making interesting things happen. Perhaps a cafe isn't the best way, maybe poetry readings or sculpture classes would work even better. In fact, the most obvious way—having a bar and selling alcohol—probably makes more sense, but tends to cause the most prolonged ideological arguments, along the lines of 'we shouldn't sell drugs' and 'if people want to drink in town, there's plenty of bars already.'

LIVING LA VIDA LOCA

Let's stop for a moment. We seem to have come a long way from the fields and woods surrounding Gleneagles, and yet maybe not far enough. Perhaps the problem lies in the concept of safe space itself. It has overtones of liberated space, as something static that doesn't need to change, something that isn't itself part of the transformative experience. The whole idea of a model suggests that it's possible somehow to carve out a pure space, autonomous from capital and untouched by such problematic ideas as money or drugs or leadership. And as that idea of 'purity' makes less and less sense, the more tightly we seem to cling to it.

To escape that problem we need to get a different angle on it; let's use the concept of the refrain to think this through. A refrain is a snippet of music but what we're trying to get at is the way we use those snippets to build a world around ourselves. Think of this image:

> A child in the dark, gripped with fear, comforts himself by singing under his breath. He walks and halts to his song. Lost, he takes shelter, or orients himself with his little song as best he can. The song is like a rough sketch of a calming and stabilizing, calm and stable, center in the heart of chaos.[6]

So a refrain marks out a mobile territory, just like a bird marks out a territory through its song. Refrains create a mobile home and, despite the image above, refrains are collective—they aren't just songs that we sing to ourselves, they allow disparate elements to come together. Both of these ideas (mobile and collective) fit perfectly with our notion of social centres as not just bricks and mortar but ways we create a feeling of commonality. Or as we've put it in meetings in Leeds, 'the CommonPlace isn't a building, it's a way of doing things.' Obviously refrains are not just sounds, but can also include institutions, attitudes, tactics or even subjectivities. They are the repetitions out of which we construct ourselves, repetitions that change as they repeat. Perhaps we can look at the affects we experience during moments of excess as refrains that we start whistling again when we hear a similar tune or experience similar levels of intensity or precariousness. Refrains are what we return to when we get a bit lost. They are what we use to lower the level of intensity, to lower the level of precariousness.

So what does a refrain look like? What does it feel like? You can see them at work in football. When the opposition's attack breaks down, a team will often revert to defensive triangles. They're little routines that slow down the game and allow you a breathing space. Because they've been worked out a hundred times in training, you can fall into them almost automatically, allowing you to regain control and then prepare to counter-attack. They provide the base from which innovation can develop. You also see (or hear) refrains working in jazz. After each virtuosic solo, the musicians return to the same chorus. The restatement (even with variations) of that familiar melody—the refrain—provides both musicians and listeners with the reassuring basis from which to throw themselves into the next piece of crazy virtuosity.

Slightly closer to home, consensus decision-making is another example. Democracy, as we normally experience it, rests on a plane of equal, atomised individuals. So it channels all politics into a framework that's bound up with existing social relations, with the world as it is. Consensus decision-making, on the other hand, can create a different world by refusing to act as if we are atomised individuals, and by treating decisions as collective jumping-off points rather than conclusions. So it's a refrain that we can keep returning to when things get heated or bogged down or problematic. For the road blockades at Gleneagles, for instance, we had adopted swarm tactics—people had to get themselves to the general area along a seven kilometre stretch of road at the same time and then cohere together and block the road. As the police came and dispersed us, we had to work out ways of cohering back together at a different part of the road. This went on all morning. But at certain times consensus decision-making meetings were called. We would retreat away from the road and assess and analyse how things were going and what to do next. On the morning of the blockade we took part in three of these meetings, each involving over 100 people. This was only possible because so many of us knew the refrain. And we don't simply mean the techniques, but also the themes that lie behind them: pragmatics rather than a defence of positions, humour rather than posturing etc. In this way the consensus and spokescouncil meetings were used to reduce the level of intensity and slow down the speed of decision-making. They were also a way of providing reassurance, a way of reaffirming our mutual trust and collectivity.

Now refrains aren't by themselves inclusive: if you don't know the tune, it's hard to sing along. But they're not a chorus, where we all sing the same words and nothing ever changes. Instead it probably makes more sense to think of them as some sort of jazz riff or theme. It takes a while to work out what's going on, but once you get it, you can join in. In fact refrains depend on people taking part and then carrying things forward. They change and adapt—like birdsong, refrains are in constant evolution. Perhaps that's another way of thinking about a moment of excess: a wild jam session where so many people are improvising that the refrains are just keeping it together or the refrains are modulating so quickly you can only just follow them.

And these marginal zones, right on the border of chaos, are always the most productive places to be. The most beautiful football is played on these margins: a few millimetres or milliseconds may separate an exquisite goal from the possibility of a goal conceded. The best jazz always exists on the edge of unlistenable noise, as the limits of tempo, rhythm, harmony are probed. And a modern fighter aircraft's extreme manoeuvrability comes about because its design puts it right at the border of instability.

Looked at this way, social centres make more sense as places that aren't separate from the rest of life, as spaces that are never 'pure' but are constantly engaging with existing social relations because they are part of them. This explains how our practices—what we do—can resonate with others, even though they might not consider themselves as part of any 'movement' however it's defined. It's easy to think that consensus decision-making, for instance, is something special or exceptional; in fact it's the way we all arrange our social lives. How else could we possibly manage to decide on a pub to meet in? By a majority decision? So by seeing social centres as places that exist within this world, we begin somewhere 'in the middle', attempting to unravel existing social relations, collectively creating new worlds and all the time carving out breathing spaces to allow us to think about all of these things. It's a more pragmatic approach which makes it harder to use ideas like 'compromise' or 'sell-out' without raising a smile.

FAIRYTALE IN THE SUPERMARKET

Hang on a minute, there's a problem here and it's the same one we identified earlier. Refrains aren't pure. In fact because they make heterogeneous elements cohere, they are also vitally important tools for capital. They are what capital uses to construct its worlds. We can see brands as refrains, used to *reassure* us. McDonald's sells refrains. With its food tasting the same in every country it wants to create its own world of familiarity and constancy, a world of bright colours within which we can live our lives. But these worlds are just a surface sheen trying to obscure the parts of our lives, and the parts of the world, we don't want to deal with. Those disavowed invisible realms are inescapable and provoke a constant affect of anxiety. Dissonant notes constantly float into the refrains. Yet in circular fashion, the ultimate hollowness of these worlds just makes us more need reassuring refrains.

But only part of this is about reassurance, there's also a linked refrain around *novelty*. It's a tune about the new, the hip, and the cutting edge. This might seem contradictory but both refrains are inherent to the structure of the commodity. Dissatisfaction is built into the commodity. If we were satisfied we wouldn't need to consume again, the cycle would stop. Just as being famous for being famous is the pole towards which all celebrity tends, shopping for the sake of shopping is the pure pole of consumption. There is a buzz to shopping: it can be therapy; it can block out the stuff we don't want to deal with; it can help us get through the day.

These are the refrains of consumption out of which we create a particular subjectivity: we create ourselves as consumers. It's a serial process, as we rush from product to product, event to event. Whether it's the next counter-summit mobilisation or the next series of *Big Brother*, it doesn't seem to matter—all that's important is that we experience the Next Big Thing. There is a sort of infantilism at work here; consumption takes place in a perpetual present, the moment of acquisition. As we move from buzz to buzz all questions of finitude have to be banished, pushed from view. We have to pretend we will live forever or the futility of consumption's buzz will creep into view. The refrain of novelty helps us avoid facing such fundamental questions as: what is a life?

Perhaps the animating force for this frenzied search for novelty is the urge to transform our lives, but it's always reduced to the tick-tick-tick of capital's metronome. Capital's need to valorise means that every innovation, every experience must pass through the commodity form. We have a whole range of potential *becomings*, but they are reduced to series of potential *havings*. This is exactly how capital acts as a limit on possibility. Capital is a vampire, it is dead, but it is hard to distinguish from its outside. And there is no universal garlic to ward off this vampiric onslaught.

In order to re-ignite this urge for transformation we have to collectively develop tools which will help to ward off enclosure and capture. Part of this involves creating refrains which will allow us to continuously and immanently analyse what we are doing—*continuously*, because there are no pure autonomous zones, however temporary; and *immanently*, because we need to search for possibilities in the situation we find ourselves, without appealing to some transcendent idea of what it means to be 'anti-capitalist'.

We have to do this because capital continuously takes our old refrains and uses them against us. And it can colonise any refrain because capitalism is ultimately meaningless. Not only is its raison d'être, the increase of zeros on an accounting sheet, objectively pointless but also capital is not tied to any beliefs. It attaches itself to serial meanings but it doesn't need any of them. Nihilism is the limit point of capitalist subjectivity. Just imagine a blue jeans-clad Jeremy Clarkson speeding up the motorway in a four-wheel drive shouting, 'Global warming? Bring it on!' We have to recognise this as an inheritor of punk's version of cool: 'we don't care.' Capital's pretty vacant.

But of course we can also liberate refrains from capital. Let's look at the refrain of the 'entrepreneur'. For the left this is a dirty word, and with good reason: it conjures up images of Richard Branson, of creativity channelled into money-making. But it also contains a certain dynamism, an air of initiative, in fact an imaginary of a kind of activist attitude to life. Indeed we might be putting on free parties, gigs, or film showings, rather than launching perfumes, but we still act in ways somewhat similar to entrepreneurs: we organise events and try to focus social co-operation and attention on certain points. We're always looking for areas where innovation might arise. The DIY culture of punk is a great example of how a moment of excess caused a massive explosion of creativity and social wealth. There is a difference in perspective though. A capitalist entrepreneur is looking for potential moments of excess in order to enclose it, to privatise it, and ultimately feed off it. Our angle is to keep it open, in order to let others in, and to find out how it might resonate with others and hurl us into other worlds and ways of being.

And this brings us right back to where we started, away from the realm of consumption and back into the hidden abode of production. The intense surge of creativity and common wealth thrown up by moments of excess always feeds into a wider movement (a moving of social relations). There's a tension between continuing this excess, allowing it to spin off into wilder things, and the need to ground it, to find some sort of home, however temporary. Social centres are one possible way of riding this tension, providing we can work out ways to keep them open as experiments. They may also help us to work out how transforming the world might move through durability, rather than succumbing to the endless chase for the Next Big Struggle. As moments of excess fade, the refrains they've thrown up make less and less sense as capitalist social relations re-assert themselves. We need to create spaces where we can continue to develop those refrains, especially as they stop making sense. This could undermine the linear notion of time that leaps from event to event, and would also point away from the typical trajectory of heavy involvement, growing frustration and then a 'principled' withdrawal when you find out your fellow humans aren't sufficiently vegan/activist/proletarian (delete as appropriate). If we could work out a different articulation of these experiences of time, it'd be easier for people to 'take a break', fade in and out etc, which could help solve all those niggling problems of rotation as well as burn-out.[7] And here we can point to our own attempts to tackle the idea of durability. Most of the authors have been doing stuff together for the past 15 years (i.e. for most of our adult lives). Partly this is because no-one else will have us, but it's also down to a stubborn persistence. It's an ongoing project to make sense of our lives and the worlds we make— and in that sense, it's hard to see how it could ever end.

> As I left with the militants I had come with, yesterday afternoon, we saw a *manif* (demo) of 1000 *lycéens* (schoolkids) The militants didn't have a clue what it was about. It seemed to be heading to the *centre commerciale* (shopping centre), where a blockade had been organised for the next day. But it was a day early. When people refuse to wait for organised days of action but just begin; when militants don't know every demo's time and place; when the cry of '*vive la commune*' goes up from 2000 on a spontaneous demo in Paris against the propagation of the CPE—we live in interesting times.[8]

TOUR DE FRANCE

But how does any of this help us in practice? Let's think about the events in France earlier this year where the government attempted to bring in a new labour law liberalisation package, the CPE, which would allow employers to hire 18-26 year-olds on two year contracts and then fire them without notice, and without explanation. Opposition was massive—nearly all of the country's universities were occupied by students and striking staff, and schools began to shut down as well as pupils, parents and teachers occupied them. General assemblies—directly democratic bodies of young people, students and workers—were set up to co-ordinate the occupations and resistance. A national strike was called at the end of March, and three million people took to the streets. More importantly there was an explosion of unofficial actions, with wildcat strikes, unsanctioned demonstrations and huge blockades of motorways, train stations and even airport runways escalating and becoming more frequent. In the face of all this, the French government was forced to cave in and withdraw the law.

It's possible to think of this in fairly orthodox terms as an old-fashioned labour struggle: the state attempts to attack the gains made by the working class; the working class resists casualisation and wins a (temporary) reprieve. And in doing that you'd have to acknowledge what was uniquely French about the whole affair. But in other ways what was so exciting about France was how events kept exploding outwards, jumping over all definitions imposed on them, whether from within or without. So while the flashpoint was a proposed change to labour law, it quickly blew up into something more general, a questioning of a growing and generalised 'precarity'. In that sense the law was not an assault on existing workers, but on workers-to-be. This opened up the whole question of the future and the kind of world we live in, the one kind of question that we're not meant to ask. On the surface the demands of the movement were straightforward: scrap the law. But people generally don't go out on to the streets to keep things the way they are, we go out because we sense that things could be different. And so rather than seeing the whole thing as peculiarly French, it's more useful to see how global it was: in many ways, it most closely resembled the explosions in Argentina at the end of 2001.

The occupations, the assemblies, the wildcat actions, the talk of precarity—all of these acted as refrains, enabling people from different backgrounds, moving at different speeds, to come together and collectively make more things happen. And so we return to the idea of 'movement' as a moving of social relations, not a thing but a *process*—and a process that has no end. One of the great pieces of graffiti from France is 'I don't know what I want but I know how to get it'. Apart from being as punk as fuck, it's also a great take on 'one no, many yeses' and 'walking we ask questions'. We don't know what we want— how could we, when we simultaneously want *everything* and *nothing?*— but we have the refrains that will help us get it.

Moving on from this, we can think about precarity in a different way, not as a sociological category, something that happens to McDonald's employees or migrant workers. It isn't just about contracts or the labour market or citizenship tests. Instead, increased precariousness in habitual life is how we all experience neoliberalism in the global north—and that's what provides the potential of a commonality with struggles in the global south. Of course, precarity isn't a 'common condition' in the sense that it will magically create a common subject. For a start, we all experience it in different ways. But the refrains we develop to deal with it (tactics, tools, subjectivities, technologies etc) make sense to all of us. And they provide a breathing space, a platform from which we can collectively re-create precarity as flexibility, as the openness of becoming. Because precarity isn't something alien that's imposed on us from 'outside': in many ways it's just a particularly alienated and perverted form of the flexibility that we initiated with the refusal of work and the breakdown of Fordism back in the 1970s.

Capitalist time is the tick-tock of the clock, the ker-ching of the cash register, a metronomic beat that runs from event to event. But when it's shattered, we re-articulate time in a different way. We feel the irruption of the future (many possible futures) in the present. And we're simultaneously back on St Georges Hill in 1649. At Gleneagles some of us were flung violently 20 years backwards to the Battle of the Beanfield (and found ourselves standing next to people we'd known from that time). And in France many veterans of May '68 were the first to move: the refrains thrown up in the first months of 2006—the assemblies, the wildcat stoppages, the resolute questioning of everything—resonated with refrains from another time. In the same way, capitalist space is governed by borders and controls, discipline and measure: yet those differences can melt away in an instant so that Argentina or Chiapas or Gaza make sense to people the other side of the world. These are whispers across time and space that can't be silenced. However it's expressed—'*Omnia sunt communia*', 'The poor shall wear the crown', '*Que se vayan todos*'—we hear the same refusal, the same desire to stop the world as we know it and create something else. It's the return of the disavowed.

If our politics is one of active experimentation, of setting and then breaking limits, then it's a gamble: we don't know the outcome, and we can't measure our success. Instead we find ourselves working with a different idea of time and space, experiencing moments of intense creativity which resonate and amplify with others, throwing up new worlds, and new possibilities. This is where the question 'what is a life?' begins to make sense. A life is made up of such singular moments, events that reveal how a particular life is individuated out of wider flows of life. This sense of a life revealed in its full connectedness to its outside shows that any idea of a true self is a limit. It's only by over-coming capital's serial subjectivities that we can begin to approach the full potentials of a life.

Worlds in motion

People have been saying for some time that what the movement needs are some real victories. But—it's a strange but frequent phenomenon—when movements finally win them, they often go unnoticed.[1]

Ding Dong! The Witch is dead... The Wicked Witch is dead! With the irrecoverable collapse of the latest round of trade talks, the WTO appears to be effectively defunct. The cycle of anti-summit protests of the turn of the century and beyond, and the social movements that formed around them, played a vital role in killing it off. Yet there hasn't been a general affect of victory. In fact you could even say the opposite: the 'we are winning' sentiment of the couple of years following Seattle has disappeared and been replaced by, at best, head-scratching and soul-searching. More a case of WTF than WTO...

Maybe this paradox makes more sense if we start to think of movements not as concrete blocks of people, but as a moving of social relations. Of course social relations are always moving: capital tries to pretend that it is a universal and immutable way of living, when in fact those social relations have to be re-established every day—every time we go to work, or exchange money for goods, or act in alienated ways, etc. But every now and then these social relations are fundamentally challenged by our actions as we start to create new worlds. One of the places where this happens is at counter-summit mobilisations: the new worlds we create there may be temporary, or geographically limited (this is the basis of the criticism of 'summit-hopping'), but it's those same limits which make them such a rich laboratory. They produce an intensity which enables us to see this moving of social relations on two different levels, one we can call 'demands' and one we can call 'problematics'.

BE REALISTIC...

Demands are by their very nature demands to someone or something. They are demands to an existing state or state of affairs. They might be explicit—when we appeal to governments for a change in policy or we demand that sacked workers be reinstated; or they might be implicit—when we insist on our right to police ourselves. But they are always, to some extent, within the terms and sense of the thing we are trying to escape: we accept the idea of 'work' or the idea of 'policing'. Indeed if demands are ever met it is only done by further reducing a movement's autonomy. The state or capital grants the demand by recasting it in its own terms and within its own logic. This is how mediation works: think, for example, of the way 'green consumerism' is promoted as a solution to climate change. Indeed the incorporation of demands almost always takes the form of a counterattack—the cost of action on climate change, for example, will always be shifted on to us (e.g. road pricing, green taxes). As the saying goes, be careful what you wish for...

But it's not as simple as saying that all demands lead to empty recuperation ('bigger cages, longer chains...'). Those bigger cages also give us more room for manoeuvre. And it is partly because demands operate on the foreign territory of representation that we fail to recognise the achievement of demands as victories. They appear as the actions of our opponents, the product of their good sense and not our activity. But we need to dig a little deeper to see what's really going on. In many ways demands involve a freezing of (a) movement, an attempt to capture what we are and raise it to the level of representation. But as a crystallisation, they also contain our logic within them, like a fly trapped in amber. It's similar to the way the product of our work is sold back to us: sometimes it's hard to see the social history buried within the latest government announcement.

There's a second reason why we find it hard to see victories in the realm of representation as winning. There's a time-lag to this process: when we stormed through Seattle in 1999 chanting 'Kill the WTO!', we felt like we were winning, but it wasn't until 2006 that the WTO fell to its knees. By the time demands are 'met', movements have moved on.

And this isn't just a question of time: it's also to do with speed. During intensive moments, like counter-summit mobilisations, we can move so incredibly fast that a few days seem like years. Think of the way we arrive at a convergence centre or camp site: to begin with, it's just a featureless field where we struggle to find our bearings, yet in the space of a few days, we have transformed it into a new world.

...DEMAND THE IMPOSSIBLE!

But demands are just one moment that social movements move through. They are necessarily lop-sided and partial, because they operate on a terrain that is not ours. We're more interested here in the movement on the level of 'problematics'. Unlike demands which are implicitly vocal or static, problematics are about acting and moving. If demands are an attempt to capture who we are, then problematics are all about who we are becoming.

Social movements form around problems. We don't mean this in a simple functionalist fashion, as if there is a pre-existent problem which then produces a social movement that, in turn, forces the state or capital to respond and solve the problem. Rather, social movements produce their own problematic at the same time as they are formed by them. How does this work in practice? Firstly there has to be a moment of rupture that creates a new problem, one that doesn't fit into the 'sense' of contemporary society—this is the grit that the pearl forms around. The Zapatista uprising is one example, but we could just as easily refer to climate change or border struggles. With this rupture come a whole new set of questions, new problems which don't make sense and which don't have a simple solution. As we try to formulate the problematic, we create new worlds. This is what we mean by 'worlding': by envisaging a different world, by acting in a different world we actually call forth that world. It is only because we have, at least partially, moved out of what makes 'sense' in the old world that another world can start to make its own sense. Take the example of Rosa Parks, who simply refused to move to the back of the bus. She wasn't making a demand, she wasn't even in opposition, she was simply acting in a different world. It's the same with the 'anti-globalisation movement': no sooner had we come into being as a social force, than we were re-defining ourselves as an alter-globalisation movement. In many ways, we were in a novel position of having no-one who we could put demands to. How else could we act if not by creating another world (or worlds)? And who would create it if not us? But first we have to create that 'us'...[2]

And here's where we return to the realm of demands, of crystallis-ing, because the process of creating this new agency (this new 'us') also involves acting at the level of 'demands', and this can be an extremely productive moment. The rupture itself can take the form of a demand, maybe a simple 'No!' That can give a movement an identity by providing a static position around which people can orient themselves—a public staking-out of ground within which an expanded social movement can cohere. This is exactly what happened with summit protests over the last decade. Most of us didn't go to Seattle, yet an identity was forged there which we could loosely relate to. That identity was strengthened and deepened as it moved through Gothenburg, Cancun, etc. In other words, summit protests were not only conscious attempts to delegiti-mise the meetings of the rich and powerful. They simultaneously legit-imised our worlds and widened the space for worlds governed by logics other than that of capital and the state. Summit protests played a vital role in creating a new 'us', an extended 'we'.[3]

On another scale we were part of exactly the same process at the 2003 G8 summit when there was a mass road blockade at Saint-Cergues: the 'No!' of the front line barricade created space in which a new body could cohere and start to develop consistency. We created new knowl-edge (tactics for dealing with tear gas and pepper spray); we developed new ways of decision-making (for maintaining food and water sup-plies, and working out when and how we would withdraw); and we extended the problematics (blocking side roads, making connections with local residents).

This move from opposition to composition, from the level of demands to the problem of practice, is never easy. The UK anti-poll tax movement, for example, never managed to find its own autonomous consistency—when the government finally backed down in 1991, the movement imploded.[4] We had been held together by our 'No!'—it's what allowed us to stand together—but without the emergence of 'Yeses' we were simply unable to move. But trying to bypass the level of demands altogether is equally fraught. One of the criticisms of the mobilisation against the 2005 G8 summit was that we were too easily out-manoeu-vred by a state-orchestrated campaign (Make Poverty History) which was used to make demands 'on our behalf'.[5]

Inevitably this moving has to take into account things that appear to be outside of it, like the actions of the state or the deployment of a police helicopter at Saint-Cergues. So we move in response to new developments, to evade capture. But there is also an internal dynamic caused by the new enriched material that has cohered around the original 'grit'. This new material has its own new properties and might then find itself with new internal problematics. At a macro-level we can think here of the debates about the black bloc or the issue of violence after Genoa, where a whole new set of questions were posed and everything moved on. Or we can look at how the idea of convergence centres at summit protests has been developed to embrace a whole practice around social centres, whether rented, owned or squatted. These centres, however temporary, are one space within which movements can thicken and start to develop a consistency.

BENEATH THE PAVEMENT...

There is a bigger problem here. There's a relation between our autonomous movements (inventing new forms, throwing up new problematics etc) and the effects those movements have on capital and state and their mechanisms of capture. But there is a danger that we stay trapped within this relation and never manage to break free. We can never entirely evade capture, but we can try to develop techniques to postpone or minimise it. And this is where counter-summit mobilisations have proved essential.

In everyday life it's quite easy to see the world of demands, of things, but it's more difficult to work out what's going on underneath. We can glimpse traces of the underlying dynamics in spectacular eruptions (Paris 1871, Barcelona 1936, Seattle 1999, Oaxaca 2006...) or by looking at the realm of demands and seeing what's reported in the press, or how states act. Summit protests can shatter this everyday equilibrium and make the intensive realm spring to life. We can see commodities for what they are—dead. We get a sense that this is *real*, this is *life*. And we can see more easily what social movements are made of. This has profound consequences. At these times it becomes obvious that our movement isn't a movement of us (activists versus others) but a moving of social relations, an unfreezing of all that is fixed. This moving of social relations is like the breaking of an ice-floe: it has no edges or boundaries ('this group is in our movement, this group isn't' etc), or rather the boundaries are always in motion; the moving ripples through everywhere—absolutely everywhere. This is the affect of winning that we experienced in Seattle and elsewhere. We felt we were winning because we weren't 'we' any more; maybe we'd even abolished any idea of a 'we', because there was no outside, no 'us' and 'them' any more. In fact this slippage in 'we' is reflected in this text: the meaning of 'we' goes from 'us the authors' to 'you the readers' to an extended 'we' that defies measurement. Moreover what we do cannot be limited to what is consciously decided: sometimes we 'do' things behind our own backs.

But this shattering of the everyday also forms a new point of rupture, a new jumping-off point. And this can be one of the ways we can escape the twin apparatuses of capture the state deploys. First, at the level of demands, the state attempts to incorporate us into its logic of sense. Here we can think of how the police tried to incorporate the land-squatted Camp for Climate Action into its own logic of legality by offering to be 'helpful' and just wanting to walk around the camp once.[6] This 'offer' was initially accepted as there was a need for the camp to feel a certain sense of security. But there was a price to pay: when we move on the terrain of legality (whether 'illegal' or 'legal'), we are within their sense not ours. Allowing the police on site set a precedent and it became impossible to refuse constant patrols, without forcing a new rupture. When we instigate that break, and follow the logic of our deepening problematics, we come up against the other pole, the state's machine of outright repression. The danger is that we get trapped in this pincer of incorporation/repression, and our activity in response to either diverts us from our own autonomous movement.

We come full circle here: the problem that faces us again and again is the risk of being trapped in the logic of capital and the state, whether as radical reformers, summit protesters, workplace activists or whatever. Capital always takes its own limits as universal ones, but in truth those limits are 'theirs', not ours. The only way for autonomous social movements to avoid this dance of death is to keep breaking new ground. In this sense, winning, in the realm of problematics, is just the gaining of extended problematics, as our experimental probing opens up ever-wider horizons. Or more prosaically, all that movements can ever get from 'winning' is more movement. And that's why we keep getting drawn back to counter-summit mobilisations like Heiligendamm: they are one of the places where the movement of movements can break the limits of its formation and ask its own questions.

Six impossible things
before breakfast

Mildred: What're you rebelling against, Johnny?
Johnny: Whaddya got?

— *The Wild One* (1953)

Alice laughed. 'There's no use trying,' she said. 'One can't believe impossible things.'
'I dare say you haven't had much practice,' said the queen. 'When I was your age, I always did it for half an hour a day. Why, sometimes I've believed as many as six impossible things before breakfast.'

— Lewis Carroll, *Through the Looking-Glass*

One of the key novelties of the movement of movements[1] over the past decade or so has been its openness, unity-in-diversity and sense of affirmation. From startling alliances on the streets of Seattle to experiments in political forms, we've been swept up in its global reach and sense of potential. At times it has gone far beyond the declaration that 'another world is possible', as we've found ourselves involved in the creation of actual new worlds. But more recently, older themes seem to be re-emerging: antagonism, resentment, class hatred, violence and rupture. It feels great, like shaking hands with a long-lost friend. You repair to a bar to renew your friendship over a few drinks, begin by looking through faded photographs of 'proud and menacing' worker-proletarians,[2] and end up drunkenly chanting 'The rich... the rich... we've gotta get rid of the rich!'

We're on ambiguous territory here. That sense of familiarity is not to be trusted. Perhaps it's just the temptation of a retreat to old, worn-out certainties. Yet aren't they certainties because they express a fundamental truth about our world? A sudden shot of realism that clarifies a problem? We don't want to lose the sense of openness, the commitment to experimentation and the willingness to dispense with tired old habits that we found with the turn of the century cycle of protests.[3] Yet that cycle seems to have stalled. The movement of movements has reached an impasse, from which innovation and expansion appear out of reach. Where Seattle was explosive and unsettling ('who are these people? where have they come from? what the fuck do they want?'), summit protests over the last few years have increasingly fallen into their own predictable patterns. Having failed to struggle free from neo-liberal and neo-conservative counter-attacks, the movement seems to have lost some of its purchase on the world. In these circumstances a re-examination of apparently dated concepts like antagonism and class hatred might just prove timely.

WE ARE THE WRECKERS

Of course rupture and antagonism in the recent anti-capitalist movement are nothing new. When the Zapatistas occupied San Cristóbal in 1994 and declared war against the Mexican state surely this was an antagonistic act. In 1999, tens of thousands took to the streets of Seattle, not with the aim of making demands on the WTO but with the intention to simply shut it down—clearly the construction of an antagonism. Against that we can plot an escalation of violence on the part of the state, culminating in 2001 with the shooting of demonstrators in Gothenburg in June, followed by massive repression and the murder of Carlo Giuliani on the streets of Genoa a few weeks later. We could add any number of events to this list—like the *Argentinazo* of 2001 onwards or the 2005 rebellion of the French *banlieues* and the following year's anti-CPE struggles—but in truth it's an endless task. Antagonism has been a continuous thread. More importantly the way it's been woven has changed enormously. We can see this by returning to the cycle of summit protests before moving to some recent attempts to organise around climate change.

Summit protests in some ways reached a nadir with the media-driven Make Poverty History campaign at the 2005 G8 summit in Gleneagles. All political contestation was hollowed-out, to the extent that the campaign's 'demands' were ones that everybody could agree with. Fronted by celebrities and driven by spin-doctors, Make Poverty History sucked energy away from any wider movement against capital. Before 2005, summit demonstrations had been at least protests, if not concerted attempts to physically shut meetings down; in stark contrast, Make Poverty History *welcomed* leaders of the G8 to Scotland, essentially inviting them to sort out the world's problems. A whole history of summit-stopping was turned on its head.

The lessons of Make Poverty History were not lost on the wider anti-capitalist movement. Two years later, when the G8 met in Heiligendamm, on Germany's Baltic coast, the explicit goal of all major actions around the summit was the delegitimation of the G8. For some, the strategy was clear: open resistance to the world the G8 represents. A mass demonstration in Rostock on 2 June (a few days before the start of the summit) turned into a mini-riot with banks attacked and cars set alight. Antagonism pure and simple. 'The Rostock riots were one of the few signals against the meeting of the self-declared rulers of the world that could not be co-opted or re-interpreted.'[4]

But things are actually not so clear. Sure, the message was unequivocal but property destruction on this scale at a summit is hardly new. And despite claims that the riot 'made resistance incalculable for the police and state apparatus,'[5] the evidence suggests that it was wholly calculable—not just in terms of the financial costs of damage (which will have been budgeted for), but in its timing and location. In this respect, a return to Black Bloc tactics represented not the emergence of something new but a retreat to familiar patterns of behaviour—with familiar outcomes. Antagonism as identity, with its own dress code.

Others took a more innovative line. Block G8, for example, was a broad coalition of more than 200 organisations from autonomous groups and the 'far left' to church-based organisations but, crucially, it was based on a clear antagonism to the G8. After many months of discussions an agreement was drawn up; one of the clauses was a declaration that the G8 was illegitimate, another was on the acceptable levels of militancy. This opened up exciting prospects for transformation as people were urged to act outside their comfort zones, but it too experienced problems. First, there were clear differences among the signatories about what this pre-agreed antagonism might mean in practice. Serious fissures emerged within the coalition following the mini-riot in Rostock. For some, attacking banks and fighting with police was taking antagonism too far.[6] Yet, later on in the week, with the summit under complete siege by Block G8ers and with a festival atmosphere deep inside the so-called Red Zone, others criticised demonstrators for not being antagonistic enough. Why didn't we make a concerted attack on the fence itself? The antagonism against the G8 was kept within clearly defined boundaries.

A second problem of organising around a pre-agreed antagonism was that Block G8's political mobility was severely restricted once actions started. The initial success of the road blockades depended on a closed group with a secret plan. With the police completely outwitted, thousands of people were moved from two separate camps to roads leading up to the North and East gates of the compound where the summit was being held. But getting thousands of people from the camp to the road was one thing; maintaining a successful blockade once there was something else. At the East gate there were a number of highly frustrating meetings on Wednesday evening, as the Block G8 'action committee' dominated discussions—taking full advantage of their 'ownership' of megaphones and the sound system, and of their authority as organisers. They suggested that those who disagreed with them were undermining the 'action consensus' (i.e. the pre-agreed antagonism) and were only intent on 'escalation'. At one point, they claimed that if they didn't get their way, the blockade would no longer be under the auspices of Block G8. In fact, the blockade was in danger of falling apart altogether when Block G8 proclaimed 'victory' and ordered a withdrawal. This retreat was halted only when two people sat down in the road in front of the sound system to prevent it leaving: blockading the blockaders!

Finally another, more general criticism of the 2007 G8 counter-mobilisation was that antagonism tended to remain at the level of the G8 itself, rather than capitalist social relations understood in a wider sense. In fact over the past decade we can chart a narrowing, rather than an expansion, of the focus of antagonism. The movement came into being around a shared antagonism to the related neoliberal policies that the G8, WTO and World Bank were enforcing globally. This allowed a resonance of movements from startlingly diverse places. The international neoliberal institutions were used to stand in for much wider processes; in turn the Red Zone acted as an attractor for our desires. The G8's response was to change its focus to a legitimisation of itself as an essential arena of governance. This allowed the world leaders, particularly German chancellor Merkel, to claim victory on the 'global challenge' of climate change. Just as at Gleneagles in 2005, when the G8 presented itself as the organisation best placed to tackle global poverty, so in Heiligendamm it managed to create the impression that it is the leaders of the world's largest capitalist economies who will solve the problem of global warming.[7] They slipped free of the antagonism we had created by shifting the topic to one so large that movement-based solutions were harder to envisage.

This problem applies double when it comes to wider climate change politics and activism. For the past three years, there has been a Camp for Climate Action in the UK. In part, this project was born of the experience of the 2005 G8 counter-summit and Make Poverty History; it was an attempt to regain the initiative, to choose our terrain of struggle. In 2006 the camp took place in 'Megawatt Valley' in Yorkshire, the aim was to shut down Europe's largest coal-fired power station; in 2007 climate activists pitched their tents by Heathrow airport, between two villages slated for demolition if the threatened third runway is built; and in 2008 a camp took place at Kingsnorth power station near the proposed site of a new coal-fired power station. Climate camps also took place in the US, Germany and Sweden and several other countries.

But climate change politics risk going the same way as Make Poverty History, a campaign that avoided all antagonism and simply disintegrated after 2005. At the first Camp the level of press sympathy was a real surprise: it was like pushing against an open door. Concern over climate change is now indisputably mainstream. Al Gore's film *An Inconvenient Truth*, the various IPCC reports, the *Stern Review* all spell out the seriousness of the challenge. This is a huge change from a few years ago when scientists and other climate activists struggled to force the issue. The problematics thrown up then have since become saturated, as they've become absorbed and neutralised. In these conditions it's no longer a question of 'raising awareness', but of how to innovate, to creatively push an agenda that opens up new problematics.

Social movements typically grow from 'cramped spaces', situations that are constricted by the impossibilities of the existing world with a way out barely imaginable. But precisely because they are cramped, these spaces act as incubators or greenhouses for creativity and innovation.[8] Social movements that grow from these spaces might form around antagonistic demands (more money, better housing, withdrawal of the police) but they also produce their own problematics. By this we mean they throw up concepts, ideas, desires that don't 'make sense' within existing society and so call forth new worlds. But just as social movements take root and slow down, so these problematics stop moving. What was once new becomes codified. It's a vicious circle: as problematics slow down, they acquire baggage; as they acquire baggage, they slow down. Rather than being innovative and productive, the problematic loses its purchase and becomes cliché. It becomes saturated in meaning.

The apparent victory in the battle to raise awareness has had some strange consequences. When you've been banging your head against a brick wall, it's hard to know what to do when the brick wall gives way. For some, it's been important to find an opponent in order to keep momentum: disproportionate amounts of energy have been turned on a handful of climate change deniers who are increasingly irrelevant. For others, solutions can only lie at a governmental or supra-national level, in the same way that Make Poverty History turned to the G8 to solve the problems of world hunger. On one level, this is driven by a sense of urgency, and the (mistaken) notion that the problem is so massive that nothing short of a centralised body can tackle it. But on a deeper level, this is symptomatic of a 'politics without antagonism', where we can make our feelings known (by marching, wearing ribbons or white wristbands, or refusing to fly) and all the rest is administration.

Of course this idea of a politics without antagonism is an illusion. Many of the state's 'solutions'—which some climate activists are clamouring for—will limit our freedom and our autonomy, will make us poorer, will impose more work on us. They involve a shift of wealth and power from the poor to the rich. The individualism of 'ethical' consumption, for example, can easily lead to an implicit antagonism with those who make the 'wrong' choices and/or 'militant lobbying' of governments and other authorities to impose the 'right' choices on people. At the 2007 climate camp, celebrity activist-intellectual George Monbiot looked forward to a new age of austerity and warned that 'we' had to be ready to put down riots against increasing restriction. We of course intend to do the opposite.

All three examples—the Black Bloc, Block G8 and climate activism—highlight the need for clearer thinking about antagonism. Yet all three clearly involve oppositional politics. Is it simply that they have the wrong antagonism?

THE CAT EATS THE RAT, THE PIMP BEATS THE WHORE
Surely we can't be suggesting that we need *more* antagonism? Isn't there enough hatred and violence in the world? Isn't there enough separation and rupture already? Yes. And this is the point. The ongoing history of humanity's separation from the commons is written in 'letters of blood and fire'[9] Across the world, whether you're picking through

garbage in a slum, or struggling to make the next mortgage payment, the capital relation is one of violence, of separation, of antagonism.

This ceaseless, debilitating antagonism is central to how capitalism works. Compared with feudalism or slavery, capitalism is a dynamic and relatively resilient social system for two related reasons. The first is its ability to feed off antagonism, to use antagonism to fuel its own development. The (in)famous example of this—analysed by Marx in *Capital*—is the move from the production of absolute surplus value to relative surplus value. As the workers' movement became stronger in England in the 18th and 19th centuries, factory owners were forced to shift from a strategy of extensive exploitation (longer working day and shorter breaks) to one of intensive exploitation (using machines to increase productivity). This launched a new cycle of accumulation, celebrated as the Industrial Revolution—a strategy which reached its zenith with Henry Ford's mind-numbing production lines. It was this shift to intensive exploitation, driven by workers' struggles, which led to a growing dependence on fossil fuels.[10]

The Keynesian settlement that accompanied Fordism subsumed the whole of society by institutionalising the antagonism between capital and particular sectors of labour. This frozen antagonism was only exploded through the fierce, autonomous struggles of the 1960s and '70s—Northern workers' rejection of Fordism, subaltern revolts, revolutions and liberation struggles throughout the South, the women's movement, black power movement, students' struggles and queer struggles. Capital's response was neoliberal globalisation and a thousand new marketing niches, as these struggles were incorporated within capital's logic (wherever possible) or crushed (when not).

The second reason for capital's resilience is the fact that its inherent antagonism is constantly displaced. Capital as a social relation dominates our lives yet it's incredibly difficult to get a grip on it. Some have argued that it's just a matter of 'false consciousness', as if all we have to do is pull aside the curtain and reveal the man pulling the levers. But it's not about ideology; instead it's more useful to think of this in terms of fetishism.[11] Capitalism doesn't need us to *believe* that commodities have a life of their own, or that capital produces wealth. We simply have to act as if those things are true when we work or consume. That's just 'the way in which reality... cannot but appear' under capitalism.[12] Nothing else 'makes sense', because of the presuppositions that capital places on us. It's the same with the violence that separates us from the commons, as people are forced off the land in the global South or, in the North, find their working hours seeping into the rest of their lives.

> Hence the very particular character of state violence: it is very difficult to pinpoint this violence because it always presents itself as pre-accomplished... From a standpoint within the capitalist mode of production it is very difficult to say who is the thief and who is the victim, or even where the violence resides.[13]

Even in the most exploitative workplace, it's difficult to be precise about where the antagonism lies. Are you up against your line manager? The chief executive? The pension fund investing other workers' savings in the company? Through its strategies of class decomposition, marke-tisation, the naturalisation of individualism and so on, neoliberalism forces an intensification of competition: that is, an intensification of the competitive struggle between every worker on the planet. With trade liberalisation, a coffee farmer in Ecuador now competes directly with one in Indonesia, whilst the growth of global financial markets means both are now competing with teachers in Leeds and call centre employees in Bangalore. Thus, capital's antagonistic nature manifests itself less as a clash between worker and boss than as a bitter struggle between worker and worker, as everyone struggles to *meet or beat* the market-determined norm (and set a new one).

This displaced antagonism is aggravated by climate change—and not simply by wars over water and other resources. As we've already pointed out, capital's solution is a new round of austerity, a redistri-bution of income from workers to capital. Measures like carbon taxes and road pricing will increase the cost of basic items like food, heat-ing and transport, and so limit our room for manoeuvre.[14] Climate change is a double whammy for the vast majority of the world's popu-lation. Not only are we more likely to suffer from its effects—the poor are more likely to live in areas susceptible to flooding, are less likely to have insurance—we will also suffer more from capital's solutions to the problem. Moreover, given capitalist social relations, the best *individual* response lies in trying to get more money (since money buys mobility, etc), just as the best *individual* response in a workplace is to get ahead at the expense of fellow workers. It 'makes sense'. The net effect is to intensify competition, the war of all against all that is capital's lifeblood.

As we hinted above, the enormous changes in the structure of cap-italist relations over the last three decades have also had major impli-cations for how antagonism appears in our everyday lives. With outsourcing and privatisation it's increasingly unclear who our enemy might be at any one time. Governance is multi-layered, with responsibility always lying 'elsewhere'. Politicians and decision-makers at every level, from local councils to national governments, can honestly say 'My hands are tied'. Politics, as it's traditionally understood, is replaced by administration, with the result that a political antagonism often makes no sense. Take the Private Finance Initiative which operates across schools, hospitals, prisons and so on in the UK: it's a way of injecting private capital into public services in return for long-term service contracts. Under the school scheme, for example, the local authority does not own the building, but leases it from a company. Widely seen as a disaster, the PFI scheme is almost impossible to oppose: 'There is no other funding available...' It's the fundamental cry of neoliberalism: There Is No Alternative.[15]

This closure of room for political antagonism has been accompanied by a strategy of implicit criminalisation and repression. Neoliberalism is non-negotiable. It's a totalitarianism that doesn't think of itself as based on belief or principle, but simply on a question of efficiency, of getting the job done. The space for mediation has shrunk to a minimum. Protest and opposition, when they do occur, are seen through the prism of public order, in such a way that political antagonism immediately becomes a battle with police and the security forces. Counter-summit mobilisations are not the only place where the distinction between 'peaceful' and 'violent' protesters has, at times, been entirely erased by the police. All anti-neoliberal politics are now castigated as either fanaticism or extremism.[16]

ANGER IS AN ENERGY
Yet, despite all this, hatred of the rich and powerful persists. People resent the 'fat cats'. The torched BMW is the scream of refusal, of rage. NO! It's a current that has a long history, existing in parallel with more affirmative politics. Alongside the Anabaptists' cry of *Omnia sunt communia* [all things are common] and the Diggers' notion of an immanent republic of heaven on earth went hatred of the gentry and all they stood for. Then as now the well-heeled feared to venture into rougher neighbourhoods.[17]

But can we found a politics on an antagonism formulated in this way? There are three major problems with this. The first is that of simply identifying our antagonist. It's too glib to simply say that our enemy is capital. As we've pointed out, capital is horribly real, it dominates our lives but it is an abstraction. We experience it in its effects, which means that the antagonisms it produces run right through us. The problem is not so much that of *revealing* antagonism, as if we just have to show people the true nature of capital as a social relation. Instead it's one of *recomposing* the antagonism that we experience.

This leads to a second difficulty, which is that it's hard to recompose that antagonism without falling into the trap of personalising capital. In the 2004 film *The Edukators* (*Die fetten Jahre sind vorbei*), one of the characters explains, 'It's not who invented the gun, man. It's who pulls the trigger.' There is a contradiction here. For us, one of the most liberating moments in the 1980s was the way that anarchist politics gave names (and addresses) to the people who dominate our lives. It broke the rules of the game. It rejected the power imbalance between rich and poor, the asymmetry of a world where profits are privatised but loss is always socialised. (Look at the current credit crisis: whilst the 'subprime' poor are being turfed onto the streets, top bankers are selling third homes or luxury yachts.) In a bizarre way, naming the rich re-asserts a common humanity by denying them the ability to hide behind limited liability companies, off-shore tax havens, and multi-layered management. It was an echo of Lucy Parsons in 1885:

> Let every dirty, lousy tramp arm himself with a revolver or knife and lay in wait on the steps of the palaces of the rich and stab or shoot the owners as they come out... Let us devastate the avenues where the wealthy live...

There are a huge number of dangers here. Besides the obvious dead-end of terrorism, this approach can easily slide into populism. Naming capital (a social relation) as the enemy doesn't offer an easy course of action; naming the rich simplifies the social field, offering us some grip on the world. But it does this by providing a scapegoat. This stand-in might be the aristocracy, the ruling class or investment bankers—any element that is seen as 'parasitic' or 'unproductive'. And historically it has often been linked with violent anti-Semitism.[18] Populism also dovetails neatly into the moments of piety that pass for 'politics' under neoliberalism. One minute we're asking the G8 to solve hunger in Africa, the next we're condemning young mothers for feeding their children junk food. Each wave of po-faced moral panic absolves capital of responsibility for the state of the world it dominates. Yet because neoliberalism doesn't rely on any of these beliefs in particular, each one collapses in turn and their serial nature robs us of all belief. De-politicised politics is precisely that wild swing between piety, like Make Poverty History, and a numbing cynicism.

The third problem is even more fundamental. By themselves resentment, antagonism and so on will only take us so far.

> Oppositional politics intent on head-on confrontation at all costs carries other dangers: sudden death on an ill-prepared battleground, or through instantaneous molarization. The latter is brought on by the common expedient of a would-be body-in-becoming defining itself solely as the inverse of what it desires to escape, in a kind of mirror stage of politics in which one becomes what one hates (the 'microfascism' that often infects oppositional groupuscules).[19]

Putting this in more traditional Marxist language, we can define ourselves as working class in opposition to capital, in order to create the antagonism necessary to destroy capital. But by defining ourselves as working class we reproduce ourselves as working class (and hence we reproduce capital). But the working class is the class that wants to dissolve itself. It wants to dissolve the antagonism that is inherent in capital; 'the Internationale unites the human race'.

Because an antagonistic relationship with capital is still a relationship with capital, it still involves defining ourselves in relation to capital. But we don't want any relation with capital (or the state), antagonistic or otherwise. We want to *destroy* these relationships, just as we want to refuse definition. We want exodus, autonomy. And this is the paradox. Although autonomy is about movement—'by our own efforts bringing ourselves to happiness'—it still has to contain some sort of 'No', a break with the world-as-it-is.[20] It's difficult to start swimming in open water: it's much easier to push off against something. Antagonism provides that 'No' by simplifying social space enough to offer some purchase on the world and so allow political action.[21]

We can't pretend that antagonism doesn't exist, and nor can we wish it away. To do so would be to fall into neoliberal piety. Instead we must act in recognition of that antagonism in order to dissolve it. Yet capital's antagonism is not easy to recognise. Once again, capital is real but it is an abstraction, we can only know it through its effects and each of these effects cramps our lives in a specific way. That is to say, capital's antagonism is recomposed in a particular way as it is displaced and bound with other potential antagonisms. This means that the simplifications that help us gain a grip on the world only provide a partial grip. Yet these simplifications have an excess to them, which we might think of as their impossibilities. This is the cramping that we produce around a problematic. And it is in these cramped spaces that we can create new problematics, tracing a path between impossibilities... and so open up new possibilities.

THE REVENGE OF THE RED QUEEN

If we find ourselves at an impasse when we try to think through antagonism perhaps that's not the fault of the concept but is in fact the impasse we are placed in, 'in both our lives and our thinking,' by capital and governmentality.[22] The problematic of antagonism makes a different kind of sense when placed alongside the problematic of exodus. After all antagonism can help tell us about what we are but it can't tell us what we can *become*.

Traditional political concepts such as solidarity or alliance imply a calculation of pre-existing interests. They rest on separate discrete bodies, with a beginning and an end, whose paths can be mapped in advance. It's as though the identities involved aren't transformed by the relationship the concepts represent. That's why we like the idea of love as a political concept, because love involves a reciprocal transformation. It's a relationship of mutual becoming. As such it operates beyond a rational calculation of interest. You quite literally lose your self in love as the boundaries of separate, discrete bodies become indistinct.

We might recognise such a politics in the periodic peaks of shared intensity, which we occasionally experience, for example, in collective political action. During such moments of excess the fictions of capital's fetishism dissolve and we face a repotentialised world. As such capital's antagonism both becomes clearer and loses its motivating force for us: instead we are animated by the affect of increasing collective capacity. We can escape our antagonistic identity and transform into something new.

These are moments of rupture, the creation of new worlds. What previously seemed impossible suddenly appears quite rational. Such ruptures are a chasm that rational calculations of pre-existing interest can't cross. The political concept of love, which incorporates pre-rational, affective politics, seems more attuned to the task.

Of course these moments often occur in the midst of intense antagonism and contain parties that want to re-impose an antagonistic identity upon you. We can't just love the policeman clad in riot gear approaching with truncheon drawn. He is trained to refuse such a relationship of mutual transformation (unrequited love is the most painful kind). We can't just wish a political relationship of love into existence. Such experiences are concrete and specific, they can't be unproblematically universalised. We'd do better to treat them as trainings in love. If we treat it a-historically and non-specifically, then love can descend into piety and open itself to neoliberal administration. If we're to reach a materialist love, we need the realism of recomposed antagonism.

Mired as we are in the deadening fictions of this world, a politics based on love can seem impossible. Just as a politics of antagonism is an impossibility to neoliberalism. But that shouldn't be of concern to us. Like the Red Queen, we must train ourselves to believe 'six impossible things before breakfast'. As one problematic becomes saturated we look to the next impossibility to give us purchase. This is how we'll make our escape, with LOVE tattooed on the knuckles of one hand, HATE on the other.

Speculating on the crisis

We are an image from the future
> — Graffiti at the occupied University of Economics
> and Business in Athens, December 2008

When we wander the streets of Leeds, Mexico City, Mumbai, the wealth we see seems somehow familiar, yet we wonder where it has come from. That wealth is familiar because we produced it. But we feel disconnected from it because it has come not from our past, but from our futures. It is this problematic, this peculiar relationship between the past, the present and the future, that offers one of the keys to understanding the present crisis of capitalism.

A DEAL BASED ON DEBT
The social relations and the processes that make up neoliberalism have been blown apart. And it's in times like this, when a system is in far from equilibrium conditions, that it is easier to see what these social relations and these processes are. Like an exploded diagram helps us understand how an engine is assembled... except the capitalist mode of production isn't an engine and this explosion was neither small nor controlled.

Neoliberalism meant deregulation, of labour markets and of trade. It meant the removal of state-guaranteed protections for workers and the environment, and attacks on trade unions. It meant the removal of subsidies—e.g. for food staples—and the dismantling of public provision of services, such as health and education. It meant greater 'fiscal discipline'—enforced on governments of the South, largely flouted by the US government—and greater discipline on workers. It meant new enclosures and the expansion of property- and market-relations into ever wider areas of our lives. Globally, neoliberalism meant stagnant or declining real wages, a declining 'social wage', longer working hours, fewer employment rights and 'civil liberties', less job security and increased general precarious. As a result of these shifts, profit rates have risen—almost relentlessly since the late 1970s, in countries such as the United States—and we have seen huge concentrations of wealth and dramatic increases in inequality.

But neoliberalism also involved an implicit or tacit deal, at least for workers in many of the so-called advanced capitalist economies. This deal was necessary for the 'resolution' of two problems that neoliberalism creates for capital. The first problem appears to be 'technical-economic', it's the problem of 'over-production'. Capital is only capital when it is in the process of increasing itself, increasing its own value; commodities are only commodities (and hence capital) when they are being sold. But how can the increasing pile of commodities be purchased if real wages aren't rising? Economists describe this as the problem of 'effective demand', Marxists call it the 'realisation problem'. The second problem is the danger that the mass of people made poorer by neoliberalism will revolt and reject what is fundamentally an enormous transfer of wealth from workers, peasants—the planet's 'commoners'—to the wealthy.

Capital's answer to both problems was to be found in the same mechanism—plentiful access to cheap credit, which sustained a series of asset bubbles, primarily a sustained bubble in house prices—the so-called 'Greenspan put'. In fact increasing house prices have been fundamental to the deal, making us appear wealthier and so disguising the terms of the deal.

Credit—borrowing—and house price inflation have acted as the necessary stimulus to growth. Or seen from our perspective, the whole world economy has rested on our ever-increasing personal indebtedness: 'Between 2001 and 2007, homeowners withdrew almost $5 trillion in cash from their houses, either by borrowing against their equity or pocketing the proceeds of sales; such equity withdrawals, as they're called, accounted for 30 percent of the growth in consumption over that six-year period.'[1] In fact the current global meltdown began with a credit crunch, provoked by the spread of bad debt: this crisis goes straight to the heart of the neoliberal deal.

A CATEGORICAL CRISIS

Capitalism may be in crisis, neoliberalism may be over, but that doesn't mean we've won. Far from it. Crisis is inherent to capitalism. Periodic crises allow capital to displace its limits, using them as the basis for new phases of accumulation. In that respect, it's true to say that capitalism works precisely by breaking down.

But this is only when it works: all of the above only appears to be true when seen in hindsight—after the resolution of the crisis. In fact crisis is mortally dangerous to capital. The word 'crisis' has its origins in a medical term meaning turning point—the point in the course of a serious disease where a decisive change occurs, leading either to recovery or to death. This has been the case for every capitalist crisis.

Take the example of the New Deal in the US in the 1930s, and the more global Keynesian settlement of the post-war period. It's easy to see this as the inevitable and sensible solution to secure full employment, economic growth and prosperity for all. But there was nothing inevitable about it. The poverty of the Great Depression was only a problem for capital because we made it so. (Capitalists never concerned themselves with poverty in the 19th century before workers were organised.) In the 1920s and the 1930s the real threat was one of global revolution, and capital's future was always in doubt. In fact the New Deal never 'worked': it took the death of millions and the destruction of half the world to establish a fully functioning settlement.

Just as the idea of a 'deal' only makes sense retrospectively, the very terms we use to describe what's happening obscure the contingent nature of crisis. When we talk about 'credit crunch', 'recession', 'deal', 'unemployment', or even 'financial crisis', we're framing the problem in a way that pre-supposes a capitalist solution.

ZERO

How can we think of this in a different way that reveals our own power? One of the reasons we appear weak is because we don't understand our own strength. Of course, when you're in the middle of a shit-storm, it's impossible to make a hard-nosed assessment of the situation: in the current global meltdown, the future is only certain if we are written out of history. (And predictions risk dragging us into a linear temporality, one where the past, present, future are open to simple extrapolation.)

But tracing the lines of our power, and identifying the roots of the current crisis in this power are also difficult because of the way neoliberalism has set out to displace antagonisms. Many of the elements we associate with neoliberalism have this as their main aim—globalisation of production ('blame Mexican workers'), sub-contracting ('blame the suppliers'), labour migration ('blame immigrants'), expanding hierarchies ('blame your line manager') and so on. The clash between worker and boss is shifted, sideways, into a bitter struggle between worker and worker. These effects have been amplified by the process of 'financialisation': our pensions, our schools, our healthcare, etc. increasingly depend upon the 'performance' (exploitation) of workers elsewhere. Generally our own reproduction is so linked to capital's that worrying about 'the economy' has become commonplace.

But neoliberalism also depends on a temporal displacement of antagonism, established through the mechanism of debt. As we said above, part of the neoliberal 'deal' involved cheap and plentiful credit. For capital this solved the realisation problem; for us it offered access to social wealth in spite of stagnant wages. Rather than a struggle over social wealth in the here and now, it shifts this antagonism into the future.

Capitalist social relations are based on a particular notion of time. Capital itself is value in process: it has to move to remain as capital (otherwise it's just money in the bank). That moving involves a calculation of investment over time—an assessment of risk and a projection from the present into the future. The interest rate, for example, is the most obvious expression of this quantitative relation between the past, the present and the future. It sets a benchmark for the rate of exploitation, the rate at which our present doing—our living labour—must be dominated by and subordinated to our past doing—our dead labour. It's hard to over-state how corrosive this notion of time is. It lies at the heart of capitalist valorisation, the immense accumulation of things, but it also lies at the heart of everyday life. 'The rule of value is the rule of duration.'[2] Under neoliberalism, if you want a picture of the future, imagine a cash till ringing up a sale, forever.

But the crisis has brought the future crashing into the present. Once we take inflation into account, interest rates are now below zero. In the relationship between capital and labour—or rather between capital/labour, on the one hand, and humanity, on the other—we have reached a singularity. We are at ZERO. Capital's temporality—one that depends upon a positive rate of interest, along with a positive rate of profit and a positive rate of exploitation—has collapsed. And the debts are, quite literally, being called in.

It is not always obvious how the creditor/debtor antagonism maps on to the antagonism between humanity and capital: it's an antagonism that is refracted and distorted almost as soon as it appears. But the everyday appearance of debt collectors and bailiffs underlines the violence at the heart of the debt relation. In the words of a Swiss central banker, in the relationship between debtor and creditor 'the strategic situation is as simple as it is explosive.'[3] Explosions are decidedly non-linear events—they are a rapid expansion in all directions. In the last few months, our relation to the present and to capital's linear temporality has shattered, and multiple futures are now more visible.

SHORT CIRCUITS

From capital's perspective, this crisis needs to be contained, that is closed down. In these exceptional times, measures are rushed through and solutions imposed because the priority is to re-affirm capital's temporality and reinstate discipline. This will be the prime purpose of the G20 summit in April (in the UK) and the G8 summit in July (in Italy).

It's important not to over-state the importance of summits—summits are trying to ride a dynamic that they don't necessarily understand, and one that they can't control. Capital's logic is as simple as its metronomic beat—all it seeks is a chance to valorise itself. Like a river flowing downhill, it will go around any obstacles put in its way. Of course regimes of regulation can make this flow easier or harder, but they can't stop it. But summits have in the past provided a focus for our energies and desires. During these moments, against one world of linear time, value and the present (the-world-as-it-is), we have been able to construct many worlds, live other values, and experience different temporalities.

But the United Nations Climate Change Conference (COP15) in Copenhagen raises a new set of problems. It's a summit where institutional actors could be forced to faced up to longer-term, structural contradictions, and dwindling faith in market-based 'solutions'. Seen through the prism of temporality, runaway climate change is a non-linear process but capital's responses so far have been based on a linear timescale, as if climate change is reversible at the same speed at which it started. The problematic raised by COP15 is how a world of values and non-linear time can relate to a world of value structured in a linear, monomaniac fashion. One of the difficulties in working out our relation to institutions lies precisely in the fact that movements operate at different speeds and with a different temporality. It's doubly problematic because while the crisis of our environment demands that we act quickly, we also have to resist the pressure from capital's planners for a quick fix. As soon as crises are 'solved', our room for manoeuvre is diminished.

We find ourselves faced with different timescales of struggle. Fights against job losses, wage cuts, house repossessions, rising prices and old-fashioned austerity are the most immediate. We also have to keep an eye on the G20, and then, in an even longer timescale, on COP15. But events like the recent uprising in Greece and the 'anomalous wave' movement in Italy can collapse all these timescales into one.

In Italy, the Gelmini educational reform law has provoked a three-month long mobilisation, marked by sit-ins, occupations, demonstrations and strikes. The movement started with high school collectives but spread quickly to encompass students, researchers and workers in education. The 'anomalous wave' has taken up the slogan 'we won't pay for your crisis', which is fast becoming a NO! around which heterogeneous movements are uniting. The 'anomalous wave' has been able to address even wider themes of precarity, economic crisis and neoliberalism's future. And another of its slogans expresses participants' refusal to become subordinate to neoliberalism's universalising identities: 'We are students, we will never be clients!'

In Greece, a wave of anger over the shooting of a 15-year old has snowballed into a 'non-electoral referendum' which has paralysed the government and traditional institutions. Major riots have been accompanied by mass assemblies, occupations of public buildings and attempts to take over TV and radio stations. In some ways it marks the return of 'youth' as a category in a way that's not been true for 30 years. Schoolchildren and students have led the first wave, and commentators talk of a self-styled '700 euro generation' (a reference to the wage they expect their degrees to get them). But the revolt has been so ferocious and generalised because it has resonated with thousands who feel hemmed in by the future. In the words of an initiative from the occupation of the Athens University of Economics and Business, 'Tomorrow dawns a day when nothing is certain. And what could be more liberating than this after so many long years of certainty? A bullet was able to interrupt the brutal sequence all those identical days!'[4]

As movements step outside capital's temporality, the categories of 'past', 'present' and 'future' stop making sense: actions in Greece clearly draw on a history of resistance against the dictatorship, just as the anomalous wave in Italy riffs on a whole period of *autonomia* in the

1970s. These movements may now spread to Sweden, Spain, France in what is being described as 'contagion'. Our temporality is one of loops and ruptures—violent breaks with the present that throw us forward into many futures while breathing new life into a past. Even President Sarkozy has acknowledged the danger (from his perspective) of such a rupture: 'The French love it when I'm in a carriage with Carla, but at the same time they've guillotined a king.' Of course, by definition exceptional times can't be sustained. But while the world is in a state of shock, it opens up the possibility for us to impose our desires and reconfigure social relations.

Re:generation

The past is not dead, it is living in us, and will be alive in the future which we are now helping to make.

— William Morris[1]

FREAKY DANCIN'

There's a great clip on YouTube. A young man at a festival is performing a crazy freak-out—appropriately to a track called 'Unstoppable'—oblivious to anyone and anything apart from the music. After a while he's joined by another reveller, and the pair start dancing together, circling around and responding to each other's moves. But the real turning point comes when they are joined by a third. All of a sudden, a solipsistic routine becomes a public event, open to everyone. One, two, three more people join in. Then another half-dozen. The momentum is unstoppable. Whooping and screaming, people start running in from all directions and within minutes the field is transformed into a mass of whirling bodies. It is a great demonstration of what makes a 'movement' move. On screen you can actually see social relations beginning to shift in a way that resonates with bystanders; they pick up the theme and make it their own in a glorious process of innovation and acceleration.[2]

By the end of the song the audience has been utterly transformed, it is energised and expectant as it awaits the next track. The crowd is searching for a new opportunity to express itself. Indeed the event will leave traces even after the festival has ended. Experiencing such a moment of collective creativity leaves you sensitised to opportunities to repeat them. Social movements have a similar dynamic. They don't just consist of moments of resonance; they also include periods of dissonance. They can find themselves unable to move as their once novel issues, ideas and practices become saturated and lose their purchase. At such moments, if they are to expand further or continue to move, then they must displace their limits and change shape. Such a task is a difficult thing for a movement to achieve, sometimes they just stall, but even so the experience of the movement will leave its mark on its participants.

Most of our activity and writing of the last ten or so years has been within what has been called the movement of movements. This cycle of struggles came into public view when the anti-summit protests of the turn of the century unexpectedly resonated with struggles and experiences right around the globe. Large swathes of people, living in quite different circumstances, suddenly recognised a commonality of struggle, forged new alliances and invented new worlds. The popular slogan 'another world is possible' went beyond mere expression of faith: 'see, another world *is* possible.' At times it really did feel like we were everywhere and unstoppable.

As we write, that cycle of struggle seems to have drawn to a close. The ongoing economic and social crisis that began in 2007 is producing very different circumstances to the one from which the movement of movements emerged. Yet we can already see the outlines of new social movements and perhaps the emergence of a new cycle of struggle. It is from this position that we have found our attention turning to the question of inheritance and new generations. Yet this talk of generations is not necessarily linked to notions of age. Instead we want to propose the concept of a 'political generation' as a way of addressing the impact that the experiences of past movements can have on emerging ones. Before we get to that, however, perhaps we should look more closely at the changed circumstances from which these new movements are having to emerge.

IN-BETWEEN DAYS

For several years we have been living through a strange, in-between state of affairs. The economic crash of 2007–8 shattered the ideology of neoliberalism that has dominated the world for thirty years. But in breaking this temporality, the crisis has also trapped the world in a state of limbo. On the one hand, any notion that neoliberal globalisation will solve the world's problems has simply evaporated. Neoliberalism stands exposed as a simple smash-and-grab, which has concentrated social wealth into a tiny number of hands. Far from being a modernist project, inexorably leading to social progress, neoliberalism is revealed as a decadent, and perhaps always doomed, deferral of the unresolved crisis of the 1970s.

On the other hand, despite this ideological collapse, the neoliberal reforms of the public sector are still being rolled out and are even being accelerated.[3] This is not because people believe it's the best way of organising society.[4] But no other conception of society has been able to cohere and gain the social force needed to replace neoliberalism. The Italian Marxist Antonio Gramsci said that crisis comes about because 'the old is dying and the new cannot be born.' That doesn't tell the whole story. The problem is that neoliberalism is both dead *and* alive. It staggers on, zombie-like—ideologically dead, shorn of its teleology and purpose, it offers no hope of a better future. More importantly from our perspective, there seems to be no opposition strong enough to kill it off.

How have we ended up in this position? In part it's because neoliberalism has been extremely effective at decomposing society, particularly in the US and UK. One of its primary aims has been to change our common sense view of the world and remove the preconditions for collective action. Put slightly differently, neoliberal reforms of society are aimed at producing neoliberal subjectivities. Markets are imposed on ever-wider areas of life, and participation in those markets trains people in a neoliberal world-view. To explain this further: when you participate in a competitive market you are forced to act as a utility-maximising individual—you have to act in ruthless and heartless competition with others over scarce resources. The more we do this, the more we come to adopt this outlook as natural: 'Each day seems like a natural fact.'[5] This is what we mean by a neoliberal subjectivity, the possibilities that appear open to us are conditioned by these experiences. The difference now, however, is that those trained in this world-view are finding it increasingly hard to make sense of the world.[6]

We can gain another angle on this by thinking about antagonism. You'd expect that the relentless transfer of social wealth into the hands of the very, very rich would provoke resistance from those whose wealth is being taken away. Neoliberalism deals with this problem by obscuring these antagonisms—partly by inculcating a world-view that can't recognise them, but also through mechanisms that displace or defer them. Real wages in the West have stagnated or declined since the late 1970s. Yet access to cheap credit, coupled with rising property prices benefiting many, helped to maintain living standards in the present and so defer the consequences of neoliberalism. Antagonism over social resources was thus displaced into the future—a future that has now arrived.

Despite erupting struggles in Iceland, Greece, France—and, as we write in January 2011, Ireland, Italy and the UK—there is no guarantee what form the arrival of antagonism will take. We still don't know how deep the neoliberal decomposition/recomposition of society goes. The breaking of the neoliberal deal does seem to be provoking an upsurge in struggle; however, the resulting collective action is socially and geo-graphically uneven. If the struggle does become more general it almost certainly won't take the form or shape that people are expecting. The vast social transformations of the last two decades mean that we won't live through the 1980s again, still less the struggles of the 1960s or '70s. Instead, the response to austerity is just as likely to take unexpected, or even displaced forms. Indeed we might not perceive some strug-gles as responses to public service cuts, even though that's what they will essentially be.

So the question arises: how can we best prepare for events of unknown shape and time of arrival? Or from another perspective, how do we, who have been through previous generations of struggle, engage with the emergence of new movements? What role can our past expe-riences play? Or will the expectations produced by our own histories obscure what is new about the situation? And, since this problem cuts both ways, how do emerging generations relate to previous movements, without conceding ground and losing their singularity?

SECOND TIME AS FARCE...

One of the resources we can draw on to conceptualise this problem is Marx's great text on historical repetitions, *The Eighteenth Brumaire of Louis Bonaparte*:

> Human beings make their own history, but they do not make it just as they please; they do not make it under circumstances directly encountered, given and transmitted from the past. The tradition of all the dead generations weighs like a nightmare upon the brains of the living. And just when they seem engaged in revolutionising themselves and things, in creating something that has never yet existed, precisely in such periods of revolutionary crisis they anxiously borrow from them names, battle cries and costumes in

order to present the new scene of world history in their time-honoured disguise and in this borrowed language.[7]

The starting point here is that we only rarely get the chance to become historical actors. We only rarely confront the possibility of breaking with the historical conditioning that limits how our lives can be lived. These moments, when we collectively gain some traction on the world, are what we have called 'moments of excess.' But at these critical points there's an understandable tendency to draw on—and repeat—the traditions of past generations of struggle. During moments of excess people encounter experiences, problems and degrees of freedom that they haven't previously faced. It makes sense in this situation for people to seek out antecedents to help orientate themselves. In fact it's a well-noted phenomenon that those engaged in large-scale collective action soon discover affinities not just with their direct antecedents but also with other struggles right across the world. Failure to learn from the experience of those who have faced similar problematics would leave us disoriented and unarmed in the face of historical conditioning, helpless to stop the old world re-asserting itself.

In one sense, then, repetition is a crucial element, one that's impossible to avoid. We can only create on condition that we identify, in some way, with figures and actions from the past. But simplistically repeating what has gone before is doomed to failure: you can't step in the same river twice. It's also worth quoting the famous line that precedes the above passage: 'All facts and personages of great importance in world history occur, as it were, twice... the first time as tragedy, the second as farce.'

Repetition is farcical when it falls short: 'instead of leading to metamorphosis and the production of something new, it forms a kind of involution, the opposite of authentic creation.'[8] The organisational models, forms of acting and interpretive grid of a previous generation of struggle are simply overlaid onto the new situation, forcing the new movement to fold in on itself, obscuring the potential to address the present and create something new. We are all too familiar with the farce of treating each new movement as a simple repetition of 1917, 1936, 1968, or even 1999. If present generations of struggle are to prevent the inheritance of past generations from weighing 'like a nightmare upon the brains of the living', then they cannot repeat those traditions uncritically. Authentic creation requires forms of repetition that 'constantly criticize themselves, constantly interrupt themselves in their own course, return to the apparently accomplished, in order to begin anew.'[9]

TALKIN' 'BOUT MY GENERATION...

Perhaps at this point we should attempt to pin down what we mean by a generation. We can start thinking about this through the unlikely figure of Thomas Jefferson. Despite being the second president of the United States, Jefferson was also a revolutionary leader grappling with revolutionary problematics. He approaches the concept of a generation by extending the logic of the American war of independence. If one country can't be bound by the laws of another, then one generation should not be bound by the laws of its antecedents. It is from this notion that Jefferson proposes, 'The earth belongs always to the living generation... every constitution, then, and every law, naturally expires at the end of 19 years. If it be enforced longer, it is an act of force and not of right.'[10]

Of course births don't actually occur in twenty-year bursts—they happen continuously. So the concept of 'generations' only makes sense if we say they are formed in relation to certain seminal shared experiences. Jefferson's generation, for instance, was formed through the experience of the American Revolution, just as the alter-globalisation generation was formed through the experience of Seattle in 1999. Generations are generated through events. But events don't occur in twenty-year cycles either. This implies, of course, that the same groups, or individuals, can partake in several generations of struggle: as The Free Association, we have been part of several different political generations—from punk, through the miners' strike and the anarcho-punk squat scene to the Poll Tax, Class War, Seattle and, we hope, beyond.[11]

They are many difficulties, however, in moving from one generation to another. Indeed we can already see some failed and potentially farcical repetitions of past struggles in the attempts to adjust to the present crisis. The Camp for Climate Action (CCA) is the repository of much of the direct action experience developed in Britain over the last 15 years—experience specifically gained as part of the movement of movements. Over the last couple of years the CCA has tried to incorporate financial institutions within the scope of its actions, tackling the City in 2009 and setting up a camp close to the Royal Bank of Scotland headquarters in Edinburgh in the summer of 2010.[12] But the CCA has struggled to adapt its interpretive grid to cope with the new situation—the economic crisis still tends to be seen only through its environmental consequences. As such the camp has turned in on itself and has been unable to connect to the rest of the population's experience of the crisis. RBS (which was bailed out with £50 billion of public money) was targeted as one of the world's largest investors in oil, gas and coal. But did it really make sense to focus on one bank at a time when antagonism towards *all* banks was increasingly generalised? It's an echo of the way climate change activists found themselves pushing against an open door around the time of the *Stern Review*: once climate change became an agenda item for governments and global institutions, activists found themselves outflanked or bogged down in a problematic that was saturated.

Again, in October 2010 Crude Awakening organised a fantastically well executed mass blockade of the Coryton oil refinery, effectively disrupting a critical piece of infrastructure in the UK oil network.[13] A real success, yet it gained little attention and failed to resonate with the wider public. Interestingly it coincided with a huge wave of strikes and protests in France, against pension reforms, in which fuel blockades were pivotal. If the Coryton blockade had also been done in solidarity with events in France, its effects could have been immeasurable. It would have raised the prospect of a European battleground, named a common enemy and opened the field for other, wilder actions. But in order to do that, Crude Awakening activists would have had to first dismantle their interpretive grid.

We should be clear: this isn't a critique of the politics of the Camp for Climate Action or Crude Awakening; still less is it a judgment on those involved. What we're interested in here is the enormous difficulty all generations face as the ground shifts beneath them. In order to participate in the birth of a new generation, a lot must be given up— often it is only the shock of an event that can complete that process and allow the displacement from one, saturated problematic to a new one.[14]

In fact the prospect of the climate justice and alter-globalisation movements linking up with newer emerging forces is not far-fetched at all. Several trade union leaders in the UK have suggested that a campaign of civil disobedience could act as a supplement to union-led strikes and protests during future anti-austerity struggles. And Climate Camp London recently organised an anti-cuts skill share, aimed at 'trade unionists, activists, strikers and trouble-makers'. A similar process began to emerge in Sweden four or five years ago. The Swedish alter-globalisation movement suffered serious repression during and after the 2001 anti-EU summit protests in Gothenburg, including the shooting of two activists. In response the movement shifted resolutely away from 'summitism', and started experimenting with its direct action tactics within more traditional syndicalist struggles.

The danger here is that one tradition becomes subsumed within the repetition of another. There is a long history of seeing the unions as the leading sector, to which all other struggles must subordinate themselves. However, unions these days have drastically reduced social power, partly because they have been unable to adapt to the changed composition of society. The alter-globalisation cycle of struggles, for all its faults, contained useful experiments in how to produce collective action in a neoliberalised world. These experiences would be lost if they were subsumed under a nostalgia for a lost 'post-war consensus' social democracy. It was, after all, neoliberal globalisation that did for that world.

STEPPING OUT OF LINE

Historically the task of making sense of the passage between generations has fallen to the Party—which we use here to include anarchist groups, communist cells, trade unions, anarcho-syndicalist organisations as well as the more orthodox Leninist left. The Party is both the repository of the history of the class, and the greenhouse for strategic innovation. As such, it performs a crucial inter-generational role, linking people from different areas and traditions and yoking them together in aid of a common purpose. Well, that's the theory. But in practice the party-form has spectacularly failed to communise struggle. Instead, one generation tends to universalise its experience and dictate strategy. With mechanisms built for simple reproduction rather than regeneration, it is unable to adapt to changing conditions: the Party regurgitates the same old line and falls back on its Programme as the One Permanent Truth.

Under these circumstances, of course, parties run the risk of collapse and dissolution. Organisations lock in energy: this can be really productive, allowing social forces to be concentrated in a limited number of directions. But at other times it can lead to stagnation. Breaking the organisation apart releases the energy and allows the creation of new bodies. One of the most famous examples is that of Lotta Continua which was a major part of the Italian extra-parliamentary left in the 1970s. The organisation was one of the few groups which seemed genuinely able to respond to the rapidly growing movements of women, the unemployed, gay men and lesbians, youth and prisoners. But when a women's march was physically attacked by other left militants, including some Lotta Continua members, the party's leadership couldn't bring itself to condemn the attack. Its women members decided to leave en masse. The organisation was simply unable to understand the feminist argument that the personal is political, and dissolved itself at its next conference. The party's paper continued as an independent publication and became an essential barometer of the wider social movements that were flowering.[15] Less spectacularly, we were part of the faction which argued for the dissolution of the UK-based Class War Federation in 1997. We felt that the organisation was unable to regenerate itself in the light of the emerging struggles and changing social relations we faced outside of Class War. At the time we were hesitant about making such a proposal but one older comrade (from a different generation) was sanguine about our decision: 'This is what communists do.' And he was right: the history of the communist movement (the real movement which abolishes the present state of things) is a history of coming-together and breaking apart, degeneration and regeneration.[16]

There has been another tradition of organisation at work over the last cycle of struggle. The radical direct action movement, based on smaller affinity groups, has used its horizontal, mobile form to great effect. From Reclaim the Streets through summit protests to the Camp for Climate Action and beyond, it has acted as a laboratory of experimentation and innovation. By side-stepping orthodox revolutionary approaches, it has been able to throw up new visions and, on occasions, respond quickly to new openings. This creativity comes at a price, however: the informal shape of this movement, with all the baggage of a subculture, can make it closed and resistant to change in a different way. And the affinity group model doesn't scale easily: it works best when there are deep levels of trust based on personal history.[17]

There's a similar tension in our own history as The Free Association (and before that, Leeds May Day Group). Our name has two or three connotations. One reflects Marx's idea of communism as a 'free association of producers'. This suggests quite an open group, receptive to new members as well as new ideas, a group with a fluid membership and elastic boundaries. In the past we have collaborated with others under The Free Association name and we'll no doubt do so again. On the streets, in demonstrations and actions, we've run with different people who have become, consciously or not, temporary members of the group. But in another sense, we're quite tight-knit. We share a gang mentality—

which is why we talk of people becoming temporary members of 'our' group rather than us becoming members of theirs. And that mentality is precious. It's the result of nearly 20 years' friendship (the course of which, like true love, has not always run smooth). We break bread together, so we're *compagni*. And we've shared all manner of accommodation—not literally barracks, but ferry cabins, beds in plush hotel rooms, tents, sodden forest floors, even tarmac roads—and so we're comrades. And it is precisely this gang mentality that has allowed us the freedom to keep trying to reinvent ourselves. A core history and common purpose means we can afford to take risks because we have a collective body to fall back on. In this sense The Free Association identity acts as a shock-absorber. The porous boundaries allow us to absorb new energy; but they can be closed to offer space for decompression or wild flights of experimentation.

We seem to have identified a double bind here. The party-form is too rigid. But our affinity-group model has its own boundaries and exclusions. Perhaps rather than thinking of organisation as a noun, organisation as entity or model (*the* organisation, *an* organisation), it's better to think of it as a verb, the activity of organising. It then becomes easier to understand political organisation as a way of navigating the ocean that lies between that which actually exists and that which could be. Political organisation is a mechanism for collectively making sense of the world, and for acting on it. But there is a radical ambiguity at its core, a constant modulation between wanting to engage with the here and now, and trying to exceed it. The struggle to resist the imposition of capitalist order is not abstract—it only happens in a definite space and time. But when that collective struggle surfaces, it brings with it a whole history and connects us to past victories and battles yet-to-come. The temporality of political organisation is one of both ruptures and loops. 'Well grubbed, old mole.'[18]

It's hard to see how this connects to the possibilities of new generations. But revolutionary organisation is about the recomposition of social forces and social relations, the creation of new bodies. The problem with the party-form and the affinity group is that both ultimately tend towards reproducing themselves. Generations, on the other hand, form around events and they have no predictable or measurable output. The collective transformation they offer means we are permanently changed as we pass through them. Generations literally generate and regenerate—and thus, perhaps it is better to think of generation too as verb rather than noun.

On 23 November 2010 while student protests were taking place across the UK, there was a march, several thousand strong, through the city of Leeds. Unusually, the march contained many school kids, sixth-formers and college students, in addition to university students and staff.[19] This novel mix produced an exciting, militant and disobedient atmosphere, which culminated, as the march ended, with a spontaneous occupation of a building in Leeds University. At the centre of the occupation was a large lecture theatre that was soon filled with over a thousand people. A portable sound system, which had played music on the march, was brought into the room and a projector was used to show rolling news. A large group of youth danced raucously at the front while the whole room erupted into wild cheering each time the news showed footage of a student demonstration. The atmosphere was edgy, almost out of control but utterly electric. The music amplified the sense of unity while cheering to protest footage politicised that unity. Unfortunately this remarkable scene lasted only two and a half songs before some veteran student activists switched the music off. A small argument ensued, the sixth-formers wanted the music back on, while others shouted them down. The undergraduate activists, who had control of the microphone, argued that 'this has to be a serious occupation', and that a list of demands should be drawn up to put to the university. After an ill-defined vote it was announced that those who wanted to continue dancing could go outside, although the sound system was never turned back on. Within an hour people were proposing the election of an occupation steering committee. This sparked an interminable and bad-tempered debate but by this time the excitement and energy had gone—along with 80% of the people.

It would be all too easy to score cheap political points from this tale, but it was, in fact, a very difficult situation. The best course of action was far from clear. The original feeling of unity masked very real fractures and divisions, and as things broke down complex dynamics of class, race and gender emerged. Yet this shouldn't have necessarily been a bad thing: it simply meant this was a moment of real movement. The protest had brought together people who might usually be antagonistic or at least wouldn't have encountered each other with such a sense of shared purpose before. Perhaps the mistake was to mechanically impose a model of organisation that didn't recognise the novelty of the situation. The student left had a firm idea of what a student occupation should look like and they knew the sort of organisation that could bring this about. But while that vision and model might, or might not, have been appropriate for previous occupations, this one was different. It had, at least initially, a very different composition. Many of the sixth-formers and even younger teenagers were not used to the culture and expectations of the student left and were alienated by the introduction of layers of bureaucracy.[20] In turn the undergraduate left turned in on itself, excluding those that didn't resemble themselves. If the organisational experiences of past generations are mechanically repeated, then new potential is obscured. A generation needs to be given the chance to generate itself; a movement must be given room to *move*.

BIG YOUTH

Social movements come into being by creating problems; or perhaps we could say, movements form as they make specific issues into problems that must be addressed. The particular shape or logic of that problem can affect the initial composition of the movement, influencing potential participants, natural allies and apparent antecedents. Many recent movements have formed around problems that might lead us to expect youth to be the dominant political category of our time and to think of a political generation as based primarily on age. Indeed many commentators have tried to play up an inter-generational tension between the post-war baby boomers—who have had it all—and contemporary generations who must now pay the costs. Those who benefited from the welfare state and free education, they argue, are now pulling up the ladder behind them.

In Greece, for instance, the uprising of December 2008 was sparked by the police murder of a 15-year-old. Many, however, identified the underlying cause as the disenchantment of the '700 euro generation'—so-called because few could envisage ever earning more than this subsistence level income.[21] We can see a similar dynamic in struggles around climate change. Just as debt transfers antagonism into the future, the time lag between the emission of carbon and its climatic effects pushes the costs of climate change onto future generations.

Some of the most exciting recent struggles have been against the neoliberal reform of universities. Student movements have emerged across Europe and the United States. In the UK, for instance, a recent march against cuts in further and higher education funding ended with protesters storming the building which houses the Conservative party headquarters. This sparked a movement, which, as we write, seems to be snowballing dramatically, with dozens of marches, school walk-outs and university occupations. In Britain many folk from older 'generations' have been inspired by these events and the students' anger, energy, determination and willingness to take risk and experiment. The new attitude can be seen in the words of one school walk-out organiser, reflecting on his more cynical peers: 'where do they think saying "this won't get you anywhere" is going to get them?'[22]

We might have expected these student movements to define themselves primarily in terms of youth, but this simply doesn't appear to have happened. Indeed one of the most unexpected effects of the student unrest in the UK has been the re-emergence of class as a legitimate way of talking about politics. In France, the recent wave of anger and protest has drawn inspiration from the ferocious 2006 struggles against the CPE (the *contrat première embauche* or first employment contract), which primarily affected the young. Yet the fact that the recent upsurge was sparked by pension reforms has united young and old workers in France. In Greece, the struggles of the 700 euro generation have since become generalised, as savage austerity measures have dramatic lowered living standards across all ages.

This could lead us to a more general lesson. Movements move because they exceed the specific issues of their emergence. As one problematic becomes saturated, movements shift to another as they seek to generalise themselves. The experience of the Leeds occupation shows how a political generation cannot simply be based on shared age. If it was, then it would retain all the fractures and divisions that we find in our everyday lives. Movements create an excess, they are more than the sum of their parts. A political generation does not simply exist; it must be generated.

Yet couldn't we argue that there is still a special connection between radicalism and youth? A recent commentator, ignoring the much more difficult conditions of contemporary students, has argued that 'Students are always first—energy, time and lack of children make protest easy.' Indeed there's a 'common-sense' notion that 'if you're not a socialist at twenty you have no heart, but if you're still a socialist at forty you have no head.' Revolt is just a phase that some young people go through. In 1970s Britain the running joke was that radical activists had three years' grace before the state got really interested in them—three years that coincided with higher education of course. Like most falsehoods, there is a kernel of truth buried in this.

What we shouldn't forget is that our present idea of 'youth' is a relatively recent invention. Its creation coincided with the post-war boom, full and stable employment and the birth of rock 'n' roll. The teenager was created as someone who was different—not yet a full part of the labour market, although old enough to be a consumer. The period of growing up and moving away from school and family life is an intense period of re-adjustment. Free of baggage and responsibilities, youth is a time of risk, play and experimentation. But discipline has to be imposed. Workers have to be made. Old values (which might have been based on love and sharing) have to be unlearnt and replaced with the values of the labour market. Where there's no workplace, the neoliberal state steps in: in the UK, even harsher regimes are about to be unleashed on the unemployed, while students are disciplined by a reduction in funding and increasing levels of debt.

But if youth is a socio-political category encompassing those without a stable place in the economy, then by reintroducing risk and making life more precarious, the current crisis is threatening to make youths of us all. The neoliberal deal was based on displacing any antagonism as far into the future as possible. Rising house prices were used to compensate for falling real wages, and a credit-fuelled consumer boom in the global North has filled our homes with an endless parade of things. All that has now gone, taking with it many of the ways we thought we'd protected ourselves. The future has been blown wide open. And the things we thought had given us solidity are revealed to be nothing but commodities or empty dreams. In moments of crisis, just as in moments of excess, the world we inhabit is shown to be a poor substitute for life.

> that there is, perhaps, some *tension* in society, when perhaps overwhelming pressure brings industry to a standstill or barricades to the streets years after the liberals had dismissed the notion as 'dated romanticism', the journalist invents the notion that this constitutes a clash of generations. Youth, after all, is not a permanent condition, and a clash of generations is not so fundamentally dangerous to the art of government as would be a clash between rulers and ruled.[23]

Notes and acknowledgements

All writing is collaborative, but the texts in this collection are the result of a process that is probably more collaborative than most. We have borrowed ideas from all over the place—some we have been using for so long they feel like our own. We have benefited from innumerable conversations, discussions and other collective experiences. We're grateful to all those groups and individuals, activists, scholars and 'ordinary people', known and unknown, who've helped us.

A few however are worth naming. For comments, comradeship and inspiration, we thank, in particular: folk associated with The CommonPlace social centre in Leeds, especially Andre, Gaz, Paul, Tabitha, Tanya and Tommo; our comrades in the Turbulence Collective; John in Puebla, Massimo in London and Monchio, Nate in Minnesota, Paul in Dublin, Silvia and George in New York (and the Midnight Notes Collective more generally), and Werner in York.

Introduction
1 'In the signs that bewilder the middle class, the aristocracy and the poor prophets of regression, we do recognise our brave friend, Robin Goodfellow, the old mole that can work in the earth so fast, that worthy pioneer—the Revolution.' (Marx toasting the proletarians of Europe at a dinner to celebrate the fourth anniversary of the Chartist *People's Paper*, London, 14 April 1856; http://www.marxists.org/archive/marx/works/1856/04/14.htm

Anti-capitalist movements
Written in the summer of 2001, this piece was originally commissioned for a book on 'anti-capitalism'. The book's editor decided that it was 'too militant,

not academic enough' (amongst other failings) and chose not to use it; it was published instead on *The Commoner* website. A revised version—included here—was published in *Subverting the Present—Imagining the Future: Insurrection, Movement, Commons*, edited by Werner Bonefeld (Brooklyn, NY: Autonomedia, 2008).

1   Karl Marx and Friedrich Engels, *The German Ideology* (London: Lawrence and Wishart, 1970). Also at http://www.marxists.org.

2   G. 'June 18th—If I Can Dance It's Not My Revolution?' In Reclaim the Streets (eds), *Reflections on J18* (London: RTS, 1999). Also at http://www.afed.org.uk/online/j18/.

3   Andrew X., 'Give Up Activism'. In Reclaim the Streets (eds), *Reflections on J18* (London: RTS, 1999). Reprinted with a new postscript in Earth First! (eds) *Do or Die*, 9 (2000). Also at http://www.afed.org.uk/online/j18/.

4   John Holloway, 'From Scream of Refusal to Scream of Power: The Centrality of Work'. In Werner Bonefeld, Richard Gunn, John Holloway and Kosmas Psychopedis (eds), *Open Marxism III: Emancipating Marx* (London: Pluto, 1995), p. 163.

5   Mario Tronti, 'Lenin in England'. In Red Notes (eds), *Working Class Autonomy and the Crisis: Italian Marxist Texts of the Theory and Practice of a Class Movement, 1964–79*. London: Red Notes/CSE Books, 1979), p. 1.

6   Karl Marx, *Capital: A Critique of Political Economy*, Vol. 1 (Harmondsworth: Penguin, 1976), p. 451; our emphasis.

7   Karl Marx, 'The Eighteenth Brumaire of Louis Bonaparte', in *Surveys from Exile* (Harmondsworth: Penguin, 1973), p. 146. The text's also available, in a slightly different translation, at http://www.marxists.org.

8   E.P. Thompson, *The Making of the English Working Class* (Harmondsworth: Penguin, 1968), p. 8.

9   Mario Tronti, 'Workers and Capital'. In Conference of Socialist Economists (eds), *The Labour Process and Class Strategies* (London: Stage One/CSE Books, 1976), pp. 126–27.

10 Anonymous, *Beasts of Burden: Capitalism–Animals–Communism* (London: Antagonism, 1999).

11 See John Holloway, 'Capital Moves', *Capital and Class*, 57 (1995), reprinted in Werner Bonefeld (ed.) *Revolutionary Writing: Common Sense Essays in Post-Political Politics* (Autonomedia, New York, 2003).

12 Michael Hardt and Antonio Negri, 'What the Protesters in Genoa Want'. In Anonymous (eds), *On Fire: The Battle of Genoa and the Anti-Capitalist Movement* (London: One-Off Press, 2001).

13 See also Alberto R. Bonnet, 'The Command of Money Capital and the Latin American Crisis', in Bonefeld, W. and S. Tischler, *What is to be Done?* (Aldershot: Ashgate, 2002).

14 Antonio Negri, 'Twenty Theses on Marx: Interpretation of the Class Situation Today', in Saree Makdisi, Cesare Casarin and Rebecca E. Karl (eds), *Marxism Beyond Marxism* (London and New York: Routledge, 1996), p. 157.

15 Antonio Negri, *The Politics of Subversion: A Manifesto for the Twenty-First Century* (Cambridge: Polity, 1989), p. 178.

16 Cyril Smith, *Marx at the Millennium* (London: Pluto, 1996), p. 154.

17   Kenneth Surin, '"The Continued Relevance of Marxism" as a Question: Some Propositions', in Saree Makdisi, Cesare Casarin and Rebecca E. Karl (eds), *Marxism Beyond Marxism* (London and New York: Routledge, 1996), p. 203.

18   Massimo De Angelis, 'From Movement to Society', *The Commoner*, 2 (2001) at http://www.commoner.org.uk/. Also in Anonymous (eds), *On Fire: The Battle of Genoa and the Anti-Capitalist Movement* (London: One-Off Press, 2001).

19   Cyril Smith, *Marx at the Millennium*, p. 165.

20   See also 'What is a life?' in this collection.

21   See Schnews, 'Monopolise Resistance?: How "Globalise Resistance" would Hijack Revolt' (Brighton: Schnews, 2001) (also at http://www.schnews.org.uk/), Massimo De Angelis, 'From Movement to Society' and David Harvie, Keir Milburn, Ben Trott and David Watts (eds) *Shut Them Down! The G8, Gleneagles 2005 and the Movement of Movements* (Brooklyn, NY: Autonomedia and Leeds: Dissent!, 2005).

What is the movement?

In 2002, the magazine *Derive Approdi* published an 'Open Letter to the European Movements'—available at http://interactivist.autonomedia.org/node/1109 —inviting these movements to address a set of 12 questions. This piece was written in response to the Open Letter and was published (in Italian) in *Derive Approdi*, no. 22, which coincided with the first European Social Forum, held in Florence in November 2002.

1   Andrew X., 'Give Up Activism'. In Reclaim the Streets (eds), *Reflections on J18* (London: RTS, 1999). Reprinted with a new postscript in Earth First! (eds) *Do or Die*, 9 (2000). Also at http://www.afed.org.uk/online/j18/.

2   Antonio Negri, *The Politics of Subversion: A Manifesto for the Twenty-First Century* (Cambridge: Polity Press, 1989), p. 178.

3   Karl Marx and Friedrich Engels, *The German Ideology* (London: Lawrence and Wishart, 1970), p. 56–7.

Moments of excess

This text first appeared as a pamphlet distributed at the autonomous spaces and Life Despite Capitalism forum at the European Social Forum, London, October 2004. We also organised a workshop on the theme, featuring Jamie King, Ana Dinerstein, Dermot from the No M11 Campaign and Alan from P2P Fightsharing.

1   For an account of the anti-poll tax struggle, see Danny Burns, *Poll Tax Rebellion* (Edinburgh: AK Press and London: Attack International, 1992); Jon Savage's *England's Dreaming: Sex Pistols and Punk Rock* (London: Faber and Faber, 1992) is the best history of punk we've come across.

2   Cyril Smith discusses our struggle to define our humanity in *Marx at the Millennium* (London: Pluto Press, 1996).

3   See Gilles Deleuze and Felix Guattari, *A Thousand Plateaus: Capitalism and Schizophrenia* (London: Athlone Press, 1988).

4   Matthew Fuller, 'Behind the Blip: Software as Culture (Some Routes into "Software Criticism", More Ways Out)', in *Behind the Blip: Essays on the*

Culture of Software (New York: Autonomedia, 2003), p. 25. Also available at http://www.multimedialab.be/doc/citations/matthew_fuller_blip.pdf.

5   For one perspective (ours!) on the group Class War and its demise and dissolution, see *Class War* no. 73 (intended to be the final issue of the paper), available on-line at http://www.spunk.org/library/pubs/cw/sp001669/ and at http://flag.blackened.net/revolt/last_cw.html.

6   Again see Deleuze and Guattari's *A Thousand Plateaus.*

Summits and plateaus

In July 2005, the leaders of the Group of Eight (G8) held their annual set-piece summit in Gleneagles, Scotland. This is the text of a leaflet on summit mobilisations produced in November 2004 and distributed in the run-up to the Gleneagles gathering.

Event horizon

This pamphlet was distributed at the various events surrounding the Gleneagles G8 summit (July 2005), including Make Poverty History's 'welcome march' in Edinburgh, various workshop discussions in Edinburgh and the 'Hori-zone' convergence campsite in Stirling. A slightly revised version was published in *ephemera: Theory and Politics in Organization*, vol. 5, no. 4 (November 2005), at http://www.ephemeraweb.org.

1   William Burroughs, 'The coming of the purple better one', *Esquire* (November 1968).

2   When it comes to connection we might make an exception for that riot cop rapidly approaching with a big truncheon… But those state strategists expert in the 'science' of policing are wise to this effect of human connection. The riot cop's face-concealing helmet, big boots, shield and armour, aren't only for physical protection. They're designed to dehumanise, to scramble any possible human communication.

3   The line's from Spinoza's *Ethics*; we came across it in Gilles Deleuze and Felix Guattari's *A Thousand Plateaus* (London: Athlone Press, 1988).

4   From *Like You* by the Salvadorean poet Roque Dalton (translated by Jack Hirschman):
Like you I | love love, life, the sweet smell | of things, the sky-blue | landscape of January days. | And my blood boils up | and I laugh through eyes | that have known the buds of tears. | I believe the world is beautiful | and that poetry, like bread, is for everyone. | And that my veins don't end in me | but in the unanimous blood | of those who struggle for life, | love, | little things, | landscape and bread, | the poetry of everyone.

5   This notion was posted on the sadly now-defunct website (Every Morning I Wake Up On) The Wrong Side of Capitalism.

6   The line is from The Smiths' song 'A Rush and a Push and the Land is Ours'.

7   Look out ahead | I see danger come | I wanna pistol | I wanna gun | I'm scared baby | I wanna run | This world's crazy | Give me the gun Baby, baby | Ain't it true | I'm immortal | When I'm with you | But I wanna pistol | In my hand | I wanna go to | A different land I met a man | He told me straight | 'You gotta leave | It's getting late' | Too many cops | Too many guns | All trying to do something |

No-one else has done
Baby, baby...
Sometimes it rains so hard | And I feel the hurt | In my heart |
Feels like the end of the world | See the children | Sharp as knives |
See the children | Dead and alives | Beautiful people | Beautiful girls |
I just feel like it's the end of the world
I walk on concrete | I walk on sand | But I can't find | A safe place to stand
| I'm scared baby | I wanna run | This world's crazy | Gimme the gun
Baby, baby

8   How ironic that after all these years fighting our way clear of 'Aims and Principles' we now find ourselves hemmed in by the PGA 'hallmarks': 'Aims & Principles' can always be modified, hallmarks are permanently stamped in metal as a guarantee of purity.

9   The line comes from William Morris in 1891, when he argued against those calling for revenge for police attacks on demonstrations in Trafalgar Square. (Although we might have disagreed with him at the time.) See http://www.marxists.org/archive/morris/other/heritage.htm.

10   The trauma zone is a space a safe distance from Gleneagles where any injured 'shell-shocked' counter-summiteers can be taken to recuperate. People plan to maintain it for as long as necessary, up to several months if need be. Compare this with the shoddy way the state treats 'its' traumatised soldiers.

On the road

Written in the weeks following the Gleneagles counter-mobilisation, this piece was published in *Shut Them Down! The G8, Gleneagles 2005 and the Movement of Movements*, edited by David Harvie, Keir Milburn, Ben Trott and David Watts (Brooklyn, NY: Autonomedia and Leeds: Dissent!, 2005).

1   As it happens even the decision to focus on the A9 wasn't prescriptive, nobody was bound by the decision, it was simply a way of focusing energy and assessing what others were going to do. Those who didn't want to target the A9 or thought they couldn't get there simply organised a blockade of the M9 which was fantastically successful and creative. Instead of energy being split, it was amplified.

2   An affinity group can also act as a safe space. During chaotic mass actions you often act with whoever is next to you. If someone makes a suggestion and it sounds like a good idea you join together. Affinity groups are just the people you know better, in whom you have a greater level of trust and with whom you have talked a few things over. During such events you need to keep checking back with your friends and then make the big decisions together, like when to go home.

3   As we start to explore affective activism just think of all the experience and resources we have to draw on. Our movements have always included cultural activism. Punk, rave, free parties, gigs. All based on the creation of shared affect.

4   Jack Kerouac, *On the Road* (London: Penguin, 2000), p. 178.

5   Kerouac, *On the Road*, p. 141

What is a life?

This pamphlet was first distributed at the KnowledgeLabIII conference, held in Lancaster in July 2006.

1   See John Holloway, 'Gleneagles: breaking time', in David Harvie, Keir Milburn, Ben Trott and David Watts (eds) *Shut Them Down! The G8, Gleneagles 2005 and the Movement of Movements* (Brooklyn, NY: Autonomedia and Leeds: Dissent!, 2005).
2   From The Clash's 'The Call Up'.
3   From Buzzcocks' 'Real World'
4   Compare with E.P. Thompson's idea of class as 'something which ... happens' (see 'Anti-capitalist movements' in this collection).
5   'All quiet on the French front', libcom.org, March/April 2006, available at http://libcom.org/library/all-quiet-french-front.
6   Gilles Deleuze and Felix Guattari, *A Thousand Plateaus: Capitalism and Schizophrenia* (London: Athlone Press, 1988), p. 311.
7   Our ideas on different notions of time are echoed in Holloway's 'Gleneagles: breaking time' and Massimo De Angelis and Dagmar Diesner, 'The "brat bloc" and the making of another dimension', also in *Shut Them Down!*
8   From the account 'Five days in Renne', posted to libcom.org, 1 April 2006, at http://libcom.org/news/five-days-in-rennes-01042006?quicktabs_1=0.

Worlds in motion

This article was written for *Turbulence: Ideas for Movement*, no. 1 (June 2007), which was first distributed at the counter-mobilisation against the G8 summit in Heiligendamm, Germany. It was republished in Turbulence Collective (ed.) *What Would It Mean To Win?* (Oakland, CA: PM Press, 2010).

1   Olivier de Marcellus, 'Biggest victory yet over WTO and "free" trade. Celebrate it!', posted to http://interactivist.autonomedia.org/node/5349, 17 August 2006.
2   Social movements have no 'right' to world. In fact any autonomous problematic automatically takes them into the sphere of becoming revolutionary. And that problematic can come from a 'No' just as much as from a 'Yes'. From capital's perspective, autonomous demands are always partial and one-sided ('selfish' even) because we refuse to take its logic into account. There's a great moment from the English Revolution of the 1640s, when the Levellers are threatening to turn the world upside down with their demands for equality. Sir Thomas Fairfax, Commander-in-Chief of the Army, loses it and asks them, 'By what right or power do you make these demands?' There's a silence before they reply, 'By the power of the sword, master Fairfax, by the power of the sword.' (Quoted by Ian Bone, *Bash the Rich: True-Life Confessions of an Anarchist in the UK*, Bath: Tangent Books, 2006.) More than three centuries later, at the height of anarcho-punk, the band Crass re-worked this in slightly more direct terms: 'Do they owe us a living? Course they fucking do!'
3   Perhaps another way to think of this is in terms of measure, and Deleuze and Guattari's concepts of 'extensive' and 'intensive' realms in *A Thousand*

Plateaus (London: Athlone Press, 1988). Demands operate in a field of certainty, what we can call an extensive realm. It's the realm of 'things', which can be defined, counted, negotiated and partitioned. 'You want a 0.25% tax on all foreign exchange transactions? How about 0.1%? Or how about just within the G8?' etc. etc. They are essentially static, which is what makes them easy to measure and capture. Problematics, on the other hand, operate in a realm of moving desires and subjectivities. They are dynamic processes that are indivisible, and it's in this intensive aspect that changes happen. Think about a demonstration: you can measure it by the number of participants, or the value of damage caused. Looked at this way, a demonstration of 5,000 is half as effective as one of 10,000. But the level of anger, or the feeling of powerfulness, or the degree of collectivity are intensities that can't be measured in the same way.

4   The anti-poll tax movement is reckoned to be the biggest mass movement in UK history, involving some 17 million people: over a period of about 18 months a huge non-payment movement emerged, culminating in a month of town hall demonstrations and riots in March 1990. See Danny Burns, *Poll Tax Rebellion* (Edinburgh: AK Press and London: Attack International, 1992).

5   For a thorough account of the politics behind Make Poverty History and the lessons to be drawn from it, see Paul Hewson, '"It's the politics, stupid." How neoliberal politicians, NGOs and rock stars hijacked the global justice movement at Gleneagles… and how we let them', in David Harve, Keir Milburn, Ben Trott and David Watts (eds) *Shut Them Down! The G8, Gleneagles 2005 and the Movement of Movements* (Brooklyn, NY: Autonomedia and Leeds: Dissent!, 2005).

6   The first Camp for Climate Action took place in the summer of 2006 near Selby in Yorkshire, UK. Its aim was to disrupt the operation of a nearby coal-fuelled power station. The camp was directly inspired by the experience of organising a convergence camp at the 2005 G8 in Scotland, the idea initially emerging out of debates on what to do next from the anti-G8 Dissent! network. The camp failed to significantly disrupt the power station and didn't attract as many participants as some had hoped but the general feeling after the camp was that it had been a real success. In part this was because of massive and to a large degree sympathetic press coverage (one mainstream paper even went so far as to describe the participants as the only sane people on the planet); but the camp was also successful in its own terms as a real attempt to take the initiative and reformulate some of the problematics of the anti-globalisation movement. See http://www.climatecamp.org.uk.

Six impossible things before breakfast

An edited version of this article was published in *Turbulence: Ideas for Movement*, no. 4 (Summer 2008), which was distributed at a variety of events in the second half of 2008, including the Camp for Climate Action, held near Kingsnorth power station in Kent, UK. A slightly extended version was also published in *Antipode: A Radical Journal of Geography*, vol. 42, no. 4.

1   This movement has been called different things in different countries at different times. It has, for instance, been described as anti-globalisation,

counter-globalisation, anti-capitalist, alter-mondialiste and global justice, amongst others. We prefer 'movement of movements' as this label offers the best chance of escaping the logic of identity. But we have also found it more useful to think of movements as the *moving* of social relations of struggle, i.e. as a verb rather than a noun. See 'Anti-capitalist movements' in this collection.

2   'As a matter of urgency we must get hold of, and start circulating, a photograph of the worker-proletariat that shows him as he really is—"proud and menacing."' Mario Tronti, 'The Strategy of Refusal', in Sylvère Lotringer and Christian Marazzi (eds.) *Autonomia: A Post-Political Politics* (New York: Semiotext(e), 1980).

3   Throughout this piece we are conscious that the meaning of 'we' slips— sometimes it means 'the authors', sometimes it also includes 'you the readers' and elsewhere it's an extended 'we' that attempts to embrace several billion people... This is not just a rhetorical conceit. As activists within the 'movement of movements', our involvement has been focused on summit protests, social centres and climate politics/camps in northern Europe. These experiences must necessarily form the starting point for our analysis. Yet the most liberating moments have been those where the boundaries on our own identities have loosened and we've started to become something else.

4   United Colours of Resistance, 'Black Block', in *Voices of Resistance from Occupied London*, no. 2 (Autumn 2007). Available at http://www.occupiedlondon.org/blackblock/.

5   United Colours of Resistance, 'Black Block'.

6   In the panic following 2 June, a co-organiser of the demonstration compared the images of the riot with the 1992 neo-nazi attack on Rostock's central refugee reception centre, which lasted for three nights and ended with the building being burned down. United Colours of Resistance, 'Black Block'.

7   Tadzio Mueller and Kriss Sol, 'A tale of two victories? Or, why winning becomes precarious in times of absent antagonisms', *Transform* Correspondence (28 June 2007). Available at http://transform.eipcp.net/correspondence/1183042751

8   Although 'cramped space' is a concept from the work of Deleuze and Guattari, we've taken a lot here from Nick Thoburn's use of it in *Deleuze, Marx and Politics* (London: Routledge, 2003). The crux of the concept can be found in Deleuze's *Negotiations: 1972-1990*, (New York: Colombia University Press, 1995) where he comments that: 'Creation takes place in bottlenecks' or again: 'We have to see creation as tracing a path between impossibilities' (p. 133). This is used by Thoburn to argue against any idea that we exist in a state of plenitude; rather we need to pay attention to the limits that capital displaces on to us. The danger in this line of thought is to see capital as active and us as reactive. What could be worse than a return to identifying and privileging the most cramped sector, the most oppressed people? Better to see us pushing forward and finding our own cramped space. As Deleuze goes on to say: 'A creator's someone who creates their own impossibilities, and thereby creates possibilities.'

9   Karl Marx, *Capital: A Critique of Political Economy*, Vol. 1 (Harmondsworth: Penguin, 1976), p. 875.

10 George Caffentzis, 'The peak oil complex, commodity fetishism, and class struggle,' *Rethinking Marxism*, Vol. 20, no. 2 (April 2008).

11 'It is nothing but the definite social relation between men themselves which assumes here, for them, the fantastic form of a relation between things. In order, therefore, to find an analogy we must take flight into the misty realm of religion. There the products of the human brain appear as autonomous figures endowed with a life of their own, which enter into relations both with each other and with the human race. So it is in the world of commodities with the products of men's hands.' Marx, *Capital: A Critique of Political Economy*, Vol. 1, p. 165. In fact, it is even more useful to think in terms of fetishi*sation*, i.e. a process or (again) a verb, rather than a state. See John Holloway, *Change the World Without Taking Power: The Meaning of Revolution Today* (London: Pluto Press, 2002).

12 Étienne Balibar, *The Philosophy of Marx* (New York: Verso, 1995); cited by Jason Read, *The Micro-Politics of Capital: Marx and the Prehistory of the Present* (Albany: State University of New York Press, 2003), p. 69.

13 Gilles Deleuze and Felix Guattari, *A Thousand Plateaus: Capitalism and Schizophrenia* (London: Athlone Press, 1988), p. 447.

14 By austerity we mean a shift in the balance of power, in favour of the rich—one which will further eat into our time and resources. We're not interested here in defending a particular lifestyle or standard of living: even our most basic needs (food, shelter etc) are a social/historical construct, and it makes no sense to project them forward into other possible worlds.

15 There's an echo of this in the way institutions like the IMF and the World Bank make loans conditional on 'good governance', i.e. full-blooded neoliberalism in the shape of opened markets, unrestricted capital flows etc. When problems inevitably arise, neoliberals can't help seeing them as the result of an incomplete implementation of their ideas. There is only ever one solution: more neoliberal reform.

16 This is reflected, post 9/11, in the long-term goal of linking anti-globalisation and Islamic extremism. See the recent British government request for academics to report any evidence of extremist views to the police. This was a change in policy: previously action was only requested in the case of Islamic extremism, a request that could have been considered racist. See http://education.guardian.co.uk/higher/news/story/0,,2244735,00.html.

17 Violence can play a part in antagonism, but they are not the same thing. It's hard to disentangle them because we're used to dealing with a very restricted notion of violence. It's easy to see the violence in a street robbery; it's harder to see the violence meted out to us over the course of our working lives; and it's nearly impossible to see the violence in the way we are daily separated from the commons. Just as it's possible to conceive of antagonism without violence (e.g. peace activists who've broken into bases and attacked military jets or nuclear submarines), violence can take place with minimal antagonism (such as when rival football 'hooligans' clash).

18 See 'Make a foreshortened critique of capitalism history!' distributed at the 2007 G8 protests. Available at: http://www.shiftmag.co.uk/topberlin.html.

19 Brian Massumi, *A User's Guide to Capitalism and Schizophrenia: Deviations from Deleuze and Guattari* (Cambridge, M.A.: MIT Press, 1992), p. 106.

20 See 'Event horizon', note 9, above.

21 It's not just climate activists who feel the need for a clearly identified antagonist in order to maintain momentum. In his account of Bolivia's 'water war' of 2000, for instance, Oscar Olivera describes a lull in the struggle:

> But as April 4 dawned we were truly afraid. We started up the road blockades again anyway. For two days, the people answered our call with strong turnouts. But the government had learned a lesson from February: they did not bring out a single soldier or police officer. I remember people standing in the roads with bottles filled with liquid. I asked one woman what she intended to do with her bottle. 'Oh', she said, 'since February we've been making these bottles with water and oil.' 'But why?' I asked. She replied, 'To throw at the *dálmatas*! [motorcycle cops, known as dalmatians because of their uniforms].' In her mind, this was to be Cochabamba's chance to get revenge against the motorcycle cops. But the *dálmatas* had not come. We became quite worried, because it seemed that the only way to maintain our resistance was to provoke the government and get it to react. But the government kept saying, 'We're not going to send out any soldiers or police. That's our final position.' A popular meeting was called to discuss our response.

Oscar Olivera (in collaboration with T. Lewis), *¡Cochabamba!: Water War in Bolivia* (Cambridge, MA: South End Press, 2004), p. 37.

22 As Deleuze comments, 'If at the end of it Foucault finds himself in an impasse, this is not because of his conception of power but rather because he found the impasse to be where power itself places us, in both our lives and our thinking.' *Foucault* (London: Athlone, 1988), p. 96.

Speculating on the crisis

This piece was written for *Shift Magazine*, issue 5 (September '08–January '09). (See http://www.shiftmag.co.uk.)

1 Doug Henwood, 'Crisis of a gilded age', *The Nation*, 24 September 2008.

2 John Holloway, 'Drive your cart and plough over the bones of the dead', *Herramienta*. At http://www.herramienta.com.ar/debate-sobre-cambiar-el-mundo/drive-your-cart-and-your-plough-over-bones-dead.

3 Dominik Egli, 'How global are global financial markets? The impact of country risk', International financial markets and the implications for monetary and financial stability (BIS Conference Papers No. 8, March 2000), p. 275. Available at http://www.bis.org/publ/confer08.htm.

4 There's great material about Greece on http://www.occupiedlondon.org/blog/.

Re:generation

This final piece was initially conceived, early in 2010, merely as a postscript to the other texts collected here, a piece that would tie up loose ends and draw our story to a close. But when we sat down to think about it at the end of 2010, of course we discovered that events had taken place and things had moved— as they always do—and how could we not think and attempt to make sense of these movements? So, the text has ended up longer and, we hope, more interesting than we'd intended—an opening-up as much as a closing-down. An edited version was also distributed at the Network X conference in Manchester, January 2011.

1   Preface to *Medieval Lore* by Robert Steele. http://www.marxists.org/archive/morris/works/1893/robert.htm

2   The video, from the 2009 Sasquatch music festival, is at http://www.youtube.com/watch?v=GA8z7f7a2Pk, while an interesting commentary, from a "hippy-capitalist" perspective, can be seen at http://www.youtube.com/watch?v=fW8amMCVAJQ.

3   The excuse for this neoliberal acceleration is the perceived need to reduce the post-crisis level of public sector borrowing. In reality talk of a deficit is simply a means of making us pay for their crisis. Take the UK, for example. According to the National Audit Office the City of London bailout is reckoned to have cost £850 billion, about £14,000 for every man, woman and child in the country, enough money to fund the national health service for almost a decade. But this accounts for almost all of the UK's sovereign (or public) debt. And it's the size of this debt that is being used to justify austerity. Let's think about this. In 2011 the UK's public debt is estimated to be approximately £930 billion, about 60% of GDP. Is this 'too high'? This judgement has been made by 'the markets', which really means those financial institutions that hold sovereign debt (mostly in the form of bonds sold by central banks). Their threat is that they will refuse to lend to Britain or will do so only at much higher interest rates. Thus austerity is 'necessary' to 'keep the markets happy'. Making cuts can then be presented as a 'clinical' decision—'this will hurt me more than it will hurt you'.

Of course, this is nonsense. While the same sector that benefited from the bailout—and sometimes the very institutions and individuals— is now cheerleading governments' attacks on almost everyone else, it's worth making an historical comparison or two. In 1945, as the UK emerged from World War II, its public debt was more than double the size of GDP. But of course this date also heralds the era of the welfare state, with the creation of a national health service, free education, social security and so on. In other words, even with sovereign debt three times what it is today (relative to output), austerity wasn't deemed necessary. This difference is explained by another—the degree of collective organisation and social solidarity. The war years and the years preceding them were characterised by high levels of social and workers' struggles. At the end of the war there was a collective refusal to accept any return to Depression-era hardship, coupled with a bubbling over of desires for new modes of social organisation. These were the salient characteristics of the political generation from which the post-war settlement emerged.

4   Far from it: only 11% of the 29,000 people from 27 countries
     polled by the BBC in November 2009 said capitalism is
     working well and almost a quarter believe it is 'fatally flawed'.
     [http://news.bbc.co.uk/1/hi/8347409.stm]

5   From the Gang of Four's excellent 'Why Theory?'

6   For an example of this we could point to the incoherence of the Tea Party
     movement in the US, which preaches deficit reduction while welcoming
     the extension of tax cuts for the rich, the consequences of which will be
     deficit increase. A more explosive symptom, however, is the steadfast
     commitment to neoliberal ideas common to the political elites of North
     America and Europe. There is a growing disconnect between those elites,
     which dominate political discourse, and the experiences of their countries'
     populations. As the 'middle ground' of society has begun to evaporate so
     has any sense of connection to existing political structures.

7   Karl Marx, 'The Eighteenth Brumaire of Louis Bonaparte', at
     http://www.marxists.org/.

8   Gilles Deleuze *Difference and Repetition* (London: Continuum 2001), p. 92.

9   Karl Marx, 'The Eighteenth Brumaire of Louis Bonaparte', at
     http://www.marxists.org/.

10   Thomas Jefferson, *The Declaration of Independence* (London: Verso, 2007),
     pp. 56–57.

11   It's also clear that generations are not discrete objects with clear
     boundaries—they overlap, feed into each other and sometimes clash.
     And perhaps any given generation-generating event can, in fact, be
     associated with a number of different generations. For example, one way
     of understanding the camps for climate action is as part of the alter-
     globalisation movement of movements, starting with Seattle. But others
     see them as a response to the failure of 'traditional' protest tactics used
     in the 2001 Stop the War movement; still others understand them as
     descending from the UK anti-roads movement and Reclaim the Streets.
     (We would understand RTS as itself part of the alter-globalisation
     movement, but our point is that generations may not be discrete.) Indeed
     each generation can have its own internal gradations. Punk in the UK, to
     take one of our favourite examples, is often divided into different waves as
     an initially metropolitan phenomenon rolled out into the wider country.
     In many ways those second and third waves were more creative, as they
     occupied and developed the space carved out by the first assault, allowing
     'post-punk' to add its own interpretations.

12   On the Camp for Climate Action see: http://climatecamp.org.uk/

13   On the Crude Awakening blockade see: http://www.youtube.com/watch?v
     =ccmXD03XVNI&feature=player_embedded

14   It might be that the explosion of student unrest in the UK towards the
     end of 2010 has already provided this shock of the event. One of the
     interesting innovations of that period has been the emergence of UK
     Uncut, which, using social media as its main form of organisation, has
     enabled demonstrations against tax-avoiding corporations right across the
     country, significantly changing the political debate in the UK. Although
     it has spread much more widely since, it should be noted that there were
     several Camp for Climate Action veterans amongst the small group who

initiated UK Uncut. For more information see: http://www.ukuncut.org.
uk/home.

15   The mood of 1970s Italy is captured in *Dear Comrade: Reader's Letters to
Lotta Continua* (London: Pluto, 1980).

16   'Communism is not for us a state of affairs which is to be established, an
ideal to which reality will have to adjust itself. We call communism the
real movement which abolishes the present state of things. The conditions
of this movement result from the premises now in existence.' Karl Marx
and Friedrich Engels, *The German Ideology* (London: Lawrence and Wishart,
1970). Also at http://www.marxists.org.21).

17   This is not to say that it doesn't scale at all: the Camp for Climate Action
for instance has managed to operate effectively at a national level for
several years but the model is extremely labour-intensive, involving
monthly meetings and numerous working groups. This itself can lead
to informal exclusions based on those with the time and energy to
participate most fully. As an organisational model it works best when a
movement has a certain composition and is operating at a certain level of
intensity.

18   This quote is drawn once again from Marx's 'Eighteenth Brumaire'. Marx's
old mole is also called revolution. It's usually to be found burrowing away
subterraneously, only bursting into view periodically. The old mole is
usually obscured because the existing world restricts our perception of
what is possible. When the old mole surfaces it exceeds the possibilities of
the existing world—the points where it emerges can also be thought of as
moments of excess.

19   The UK government is attempting to impose widespread educational
reform, including: increased marketisation of higher education, the
tripling of university tuition fees and the abolition of the EMA, an
allowance paid to 16–18 year-olds (sixth-formers) who remain in
education.

20   Of course they might have found the introduction of a complex consensus
decision-making process just as off-putting at that point.

21   It has now been downgraded to the '600 euro generation', as the post-
crisis austerity has lowered living standards even more. *We Are An Image
From the Future*, edited by A.G. Schwarz, Tasos Sagris and Void Network
(Oakland and Edinburgh: AK Press 2010), is an indispensable account of
the Greek revolt of December 2008, while http://www.occupiedlondon.
org/blog/ is an inspirational example of online publishing.

22   This was quoted in the *Guardian* on 19 November, 2010. There is a
nice twist here: the organiser turned out to be the son of a friend
of ours, a political activist involved in several previous generations
of struggle. See: http://www.guardian.co.uk/world/2010/nov/19/
pupilswalk-out-tuition-fees?intcmp=239

23   We've taken this quotation from the back cover of the Clash's first single
'White Riot'/'1977', although it's originally from Stuart Christie and Albert
Meltzer's 1970 book *The Floodgates of Anarchy*.

About the authors

The Free Association is an ongoing experiment—a reading collective, a writing machine, an affinity group. Most of its members are based in Leeds, England, and their political history and friendship date back to the early 1990s. Alex Dennis, David Harvie, Nette, Keir Milburn and David Watts freely associated to produce the texts here. More information can be found at http://freelyassociating.org/

ABOUT PM PRESS

PM Press was founded at the end of 2007
by a small collection of folks with decades of
publishing, media, and organizing experience.
PM Press co-conspirators have published and
distributed hundreds of books, pamphlets,
CDs, and DVDs. Members of PM have founded

enduring book fairs, spearheaded victorious tenant organizing campaigns,
and worked closely with bookstores, academic conferences, and even rock
bands to deliver political and challenging ideas to all walks of life. We're
old enough to know what we're doing and young enough to know what's
at stake.

We seek to create radical and stimulating fiction and non-fiction books,
pamphlets, t-shirts, visual and audio materials to entertain, educate and
inspire you. We aim to distribute these through every available channel
with every available technology—whether that means you are seeing
anarchist classics at our bookfair stalls; reading our latest vegan cookbook
at the café; downloading geeky fiction e-books; or digging new music and
timely videos from our website.

PM Press is always on the lookout for talented and skilled volunteers,
artists, activists and writers to work with. If you have a great idea for a
project or can contribute in some way, please get in touch.

PM Press
PO Box 23912
Oakland, CA 94623
www.pmpress.org

FRIENDS OF PM PRESS

These are indisputably momentous times—the financial system is melting down globally and the Empire is stumbling. Now more than ever there is a vital need for radical ideas.

In the three years since its founding—and on a mere shoestring—PM Press has risen to the formidable challenge of publishing and distributing knowledge and entertainment for the struggles ahead. With over 100 releases to date, we have published an impressive and stimulating array of literature, art, music, politics, and culture. Using every available medium, we've succeeded in connecting those hungry for ideas and information to those putting them into practice.

Friends of PM allows you to directly help impact, amplify, and revitalize the discourse and actions of radical writers, filmmakers, and artists. It provides us with a stable foundation from which we can build upon our early successes and provides a much-needed subsidy for the materials that can't necessarily pay their own way. You can help make that happen—and receive every new title automatically delivered to your door once a month—by joining as a Friend of PM Press. And, we'll throw in a free T-Shirt when you sign up.

Here are your options:

- **$25 a month** Get all books and pamphlets plus 50% discount on all webstore purchases
- **$25 a month** Get all CDs and DVDs plus 50% discount on all webstore purchases
- **$40 a month** Get all PM Press releases plus 50% discount on all webstore purchases
- **$100 a month** Superstar — Everything plus PM merchandise, free downloads, and 50% discount on all webstore purchases

For those who can't afford $25 or more a month, we're introducing **Sustainer Rates** at $15, $10 and $5. Sustainers get a free PM Press t-shirt and a 50% discount on all purchases from our website.

Your Visa or Mastercard will be billed once a month, until you tell us to stop. Or until our efforts succeed in bringing the revolution around. Or the financial meltdown of Capital makes plastic redundant. Whichever comes first.

What Would It Mean to Win?

Turbulence Collective

ISBN: 978-1-60486-110-5
$14.95   160 pages

Movements become apparent as "movements" at times of acceleration and expansion. In these heady moments they have fuzzy boundaries, no membership lists—everybody is too engaged in what's coming next, in creating the new, looking to the horizon. But movements get blocked, they slow down, they cease to move, or continue to move without considering their actual effects. When this happens, they can stifle new developments, suppress the emergence of new forms of politics; or fail to see other possible directions. Many movements just stop functioning as movements. They become those strange political groups of yesteryear, arguing about history as worlds pass by. Sometimes all it takes to get moving again is a nudge in a new direction... We think now is a good time to ask the question: What is winning? Or: What would—or could—it mean to "win?"

Contributors include: Valery Alzaga and Rodrigo Nunes, Colectivo Situaciones, Stephen Duncombe, Gustavo Esteva, The Free Association, Euclides André Mance, Michal Osterweil, Sasha Lilley, Kay Summer and Harry Halpin, Ben Trott, and Nick Dyer-Witheford and more.

This edition includes a foreword by John Holloway and an extended interview with Michal Osterweil and Ben Trott of the Turbulence Collective.

"*Where is the movement today? Where is it going? Are we winning? The authors of the essays in this volume pose these and other momentous questions. There are no easy answers, but the discussion is always insightful and provocative as the writers bravely take on the challenge of charting the directions for the Left at a time of ecological crisis, economic collapse, and political disillusionment.*"
—Walden Bello, Executive Director of Focus on the Global South

"*Turbulence presents an exciting brand of political theorising that is directed and inspired by current strategic questions for activism. This kind of innovative thinking, which emerges from the context of the movements, opens new paths for rebellion and the creation of real social alternatives.*"
—Michael Hardt, co-author of *Commonwealth*, *Multitude* and *Empire*.

"*The history of the past half-century and particularly the last decade is as easily told as a series of victories as defeats, maybe best as both. Sometimes we won—and this is what makes the* What Does It Mean to Win? *anthology such a powerful vision of the possible and the seldom-seen present.*
—Rebecca Solnit, author of *Hope in the Dark* and *A Paradise Built in Hell*.

Also from SPECTRE CLASSICS from PM Press

William Morris: Romantic to Revolutionary

E. P. Thompson

ISBN: 978-1-60486-243-0
$32.95   880 pages

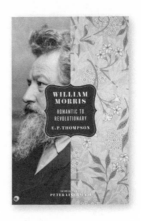

William Morris—the great 19th-century craftsman, architect, designer, poet and writer—remains a monumental figure whose influence resonates powerfully today. As an intellectual (and author of the seminal utopian *News From Nowhere*), his concern with artistic and human values led him to cross what he called the "river of fire" and become a committed socialist—committed not to some theoretical formula but to the day-by-day struggle of working women and men in Britain and to the evolution of his ideas about art, about work and about how life should be lived. Many of his ideas accorded none too well with the reforming tendencies dominant in the Labour movement, nor with those of "orthodox" Marxism, which has looked elsewhere for inspiration. Both sides have been inclined to venerate Morris rather than to pay attention to what he said. Originally written less than a decade before his groundbreaking *The Making of the English Working Class*, E. P. Thompson brought to this biography his now trademark historical mastery, passion, wit, and essential sympathy. It remains unsurpassed as the definitive work on this remarkable figure, by the major British historian of the 20th century.

"Two impressive figures, William Morris as subject and E. P. Thompson as author, are conjoined in this immense biographical-historical-critical study, and both of them have gained in stature since the first edition of the book was published... The book that was ignored in 1955 has meanwhile become something of an underground classic—almost impossible to locate in second-hand bookstores, pored over in libraries, required reading for anyone interested in Morris and, increasingly, for anyone interested in one of the most important of contemporary British historians... Thompson has the distinguishing characteristic of a great historian: he has transformed the nature of the past, it will never look the same again; and whoever works in the area of his concerns in the future must come to terms with what Thompson has written. So too with his study of William Morris."
—Peter Stansky, *The New York Times Book Review*

"An absorbing biographical study... A glittering quarry of marvelous quotes from Morris and others, many taken from heretofore inaccessible or unpublished sources."
—Walter Arnold, *Saturday Review*

A New Notion:
Two Works by C. L. R. James
"Every Cook Can Govern" and
"The Invading Socialist Society"
Edited by Noel Ignatiev

ISBN: 978-1-60486-047-4
$16.95 160 pages

C. L. R. James was a leading figure in the independence movement in the West Indies, and the black and working-class movements in both Britain and the United States. As a major contributor to Marxist and revolutionary theory, his project was to discover, document, and elaborate the aspects of working-class activity that constitute the revolution in today's world. In this volume, Noel Ignatiev, author of *How the Irish Became White*, provides an extensive introduction to James' life and thought, before presenting two critical works that together illustrate the tremendous breadth and depth of James' worldview. "The Invading Socialist Society," for James the fundamental document of his political tendency, shows clearly the power of James's political acumen and its relevance in today's world with a clarity of analysis that anticipated future events to a remarkable extent. "Every Cook Can Govern," is a short and eminently readable piece counterpoising direct with representative democracy, and getting to the heart of how we should relate to one another. Together these two works represent the principal themes that run through James's life: implacable hostility toward all "condescending saviors" of the working class, and undying faith in the power of ordinary people to build a new world.

"It would take a person with great confidence, and good judgment, to select from the substantial writings of C. L. R. James just two items to represent the 'principal themes' in James' life and thought. Fortunately, Noel Ignatiev is such a person. With a concise, but thorough introduction, Ignatiev sets the stage and C. L. R. James does the rest. In these often confusing times one way to keep one's head on straight and to chart a clear path to the future is to engage the analytical methods and theoretical insights of C. L. R. James. What you hold in your hands is an excellent starting point."
—John H. Bracey Jr., professor of African-American Studies at the University of Massachusetts–Amherst and co-editor of *Strangers & Neighbors: Relations Between Blacks & Jews in the United States.*

"C. L. R. James has arguably had a greater influence on the underlying thinking of independence movements in the West Indies and Africa than any living man."
—*Sunday Times*

Wobblies and Zapatistas: Conversations on Anarchism, Marxism and Radical History

Staughton Lynd and Andrej Grubačić

ISBN: 978-1-60486-041-2
$20.00   300 pages

Wobblies and Zapatistas offers the reader an encounter between two generations and two traditions. Andrej Grubačić is an anarchist from the Balkans. Staughton Lynd is a lifelong pacifist, influenced by Marxism. They meet in dialogue in an effort to bring together the anarchist and Marxist traditions, to discuss the writing of history by those who make it, and to remind us of the idea that "my country is the world." Encompassing a Left libertarian perspective and an emphatically activist standpoint, these conversations are meant to be read in the clubs and affinity groups of the new Movement. The authors accompany us on a journey through modern revolutions, direct actions, anti-globalist counter summits, Freedom Schools, Zapatista cooperatives, Haymarket and Petrograd, Hanoi and Belgrade, "intentional" communities, wildcat strikes, early Protestant communities, Native American democratic practices, the Workers' Solidarity Club of Youngstown, occupied factories, self-organized councils and soviets, the lives of forgotten revolutionaries, Quaker meetings, antiwar movements, and prison rebellions. Neglected and forgotten moments of interracial self-activity are brought to light. The book invites the attention of readers who believe that a better world, on the other side of capitalism and state bureaucracy, may indeed be possible.

"There's no doubt that we've lost much of our history. It's also very clear that those in power in this country like it that way. Here's a book that shows us why. It demonstrates not only that another world is possible, but that it already exists, has existed, and shows an endless potential to burst through the artificial walls and divisions that currently imprison us. An exquisite contribution to the literature of human freedom, and coming not a moment too soon."
—David Graeber, author of *Fragments of an Anarchist Anthropology* and *Direct Action: An Ethnography*

"I have been in regular contact with Andrej Grubačić for many years, and have been most impressed by his searching intelligence, broad knowledge, lucid judgment, and penetrating commentary on contemporary affairs and their historical roots. He is an original thinker and dedicated activist, who brings deep understanding and outstanding personal qualities to everything he does."
—Noam Chomsky

Also from ■SPECTRE▶ from PM Press

Global Slump: The Economics and Politics of Crisis and Resistance

David McNally

ISBN: 978-1-60486-332-1
$15.95 176 pages

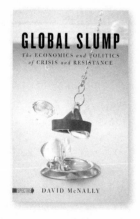

Global Slump analyzes the world financial meltdown as the first systemic crisis of the neoliberal stage of capitalism. It argues that—far from having ended—the crisis has ushered in a whole period of worldwide economic and political turbulence. In developing an account of the crisis as rooted in fundamental features of capitalism, Global Slump challenges the view that its source lies in financial deregulation. It offers an original account of the "financialization" of the world economy and explores the connections between international financial markets and new forms of debt and dispossession, particularly in the Global South. The book shows that, while averting a complete meltdown, the massive intervention by central banks laid the basis for recurring crises for poor and working class people. It traces new patterns of social resistance for building an anti-capitalist opposition to the damage that neoliberal capitalism is inflicting on the lives of millions.

"In this book, McNally confirms—once again—his standing as one of the world's leading Marxist scholars of capitalism. For a scholarly, in depth analysis of our current crisis that never loses sight of its political implications (for them and for us), expressed in a language that leaves no reader behind, there is simply no better place to go."
—Bertell Ollman, professor, Department of Politics, NYU, and author of Dance of the Dialectic: Steps in Marx's Method

"David McNally's tremendously timely book is packed with significant theoretical and practical insights, and offers actually-existing examples of what is to be done. Global Slump urgently details how changes in the capitalist space-economy over the past 25 years, especially in the forms that money takes, have expanded wide-scale vulnerabilities for all kinds of people, and how people fight back. In a word, the problem isn't neo-liberalism—it's capitalism."
—Ruth Wilson Gilmore, University of Southern California and author, Golden Gulag

In and Out of Crisis: The Global Financial Meltdown and Left Alternatives

Greg Albo, Sam Gindin, Leo Panitch

ISBN: 978-1-60486-212-6
$13.95 144 pages

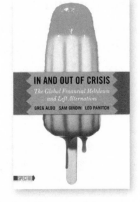

While many around the globe are increasingly wondering if another world is indeed possible, few are mapping out potential avenues—and flagging wrong turns—en route to a post-capitalist future. In this groundbreaking analysis of the meltdown, renowned radical political economists Albo, Gindin, and Panitch lay bare the roots of the crisis, which they locate in the dynamic expansion of capital on a global scale over the last quarter century—and in the inner logic of capitalism itself.

With an unparalleled understanding of the inner workings of capitalism, the authors of *In and Out of Crisis* provocatively challenge the call by much of the Left for a return to a largely mythical Golden Age of economic regulation as a check on finance capital unbound. They deftly illuminate how the era of neoliberal free markets has been, in practice, undergirded by state intervention on a massive scale. In conclusion, the authors argue that it's time to start thinking about genuinely transformative alternatives to capitalism—and how to build the collective capacity to get us there. *In and Out of Crisis* stands to be the enduring critique of the crisis and an indispensable springboard for a renewed Left.

"Once again, Panitch, Gindin, and Albo show that they have few rivals and no betters in analyzing the relations between politics and economics, between globalization and American power, between theory and quotidian reality, and between crisis and political possibility. At once sobering and inspiring, this is one of the few pieces of writing that I've seen that's essential to understanding—to paraphrase a term from accounting— the sources and uses of crisis. Splendid and essential."
—Doug Henwood, *Left Business Observer*, author of *After the New Economy* and *Wall Street*

"Mired in political despair? Planning your escape to a more humane continent? Baffled by the economy? Convinced that the Left is out of ideas? Pull yourself together and read this book, in which Albo, Gindin, and Panitch, some of the world's sharpest living political economists, explain the current financial crisis—and how we might begin to make a better world."
—Liza Featherstone, author of *Students Against Sweatshops* and *Selling Women Short: The Landmark Battle for Worker's Rights at Wal-Mart*

Capital and Its Discontents: Conversations with Radical Thinkers in a Time of Tumult

Sasha Lilley

ISBN: 978-1-60486-334-5
$20.00   320 pages

Capitalism is stumbling, empire is faltering, and the planet is thawing. Yet many people are still grasping to understand these multiple crises and to find a way forward to a just future. Into the breach come the essential insights of *Capital and Its Discontents*, which cut through the gristle to get to the heart of the matter about the nature of capitalism and imperialism, capitalism's vulnerabilities at this conjuncture—and what we can do to hasten its demise. Through a series of incisive conversations with some of the most eminent thinkers and political economists on the Left—including David Harvey, Ellen Meiksins Wood, Mike Davis, Leo Panitch, Tariq Ali, and Noam Chomsky—*Capital and Its Discontents* illuminates the dynamic contradictions undergirding capitalism and the potential for its dethroning. At a moment when capitalism as a system is more reviled than ever, here is an indispensable toolbox of ideas for action by some of the most brilliant thinkers of our times.

"*These conversations illuminate the current world situation in ways that are very useful for those hoping to orient themselves and find a way forward to effective individual and collective action. Highly recommended.*"
—Kim Stanley Robinson, *New York Times* bestselling author of the *Mars Trilogy* and *The Years of Rice and Salt*

"*In this fine set of interviews, an A-list of radical political economists demonstrate why their skills are indispensable to understanding today's multiple economic and ecological crises.*"
—Raj Patel, author of *Stuffed and Starved* and *The Value of Nothing*

"*This is an extremely important book. It is the most detailed, comprehensive, and best study yet published on the most recent capitalist crisis and its discontents. Sasha Lilley sets each interview in its context, writing with style, scholarship, and wit about ideas and philosophies.*"
—Andrej Grubačić, radical sociologist and social critic, co-author of *Wobblies and Zapatistas*